ILLUMINATIONS

RIMBAUD

ILLUMINATIONS

and

Other Prose Poems

TRANSLATED BY

LOUISE VARÈSE

REVISED EDITION

A NEW DIRECTIONS PAPERBOOK

TWENTIETH PRINTING

CONTENTS

INTRODUCTION   vii

BY WAY OF A PREFACE (*Les Lettres du Voyant*)   xxv

Illuminations (*Illuminations*)

AFTER THE DELUGE (*Après le Déluge*)   2

CHILDHOOD (*Enfance*)   6

TALE (*Conte*)   16

SIDE SHOW (*Parade*)   20

ANTIQUE (*Antique*)   24

BEAUTEOUS BEING (*Being Beauteous*)   26

LIVES (*Vies*)   28

DEPARTURE (*Départ*)   34

ROYALTY (*Royauté*)   36

TO A REASON (*A une Raison*)   38

MORNING OF DRUNKENNESS (*Matinée d'Ivresse*)   40

PHRASES (*Phrases*)   44

WORKING PEOPLE (*Ouvriers*)   50

THE BRIDGES (*Les Ponts*)   54

CITY (*Ville*)   56

RUTS (*Ornières*)   58

CITIES (*Villes*)   60

VAGABONDS (*Vagabonds*)   64

CONTENTS

CITIES (*Villes*)   68

VIGILS (*Veillées*)   74

MYSTIC (*Mystique*)   78

DAWN (*Aube*)   80

FLOWERS (*Fleurs*)   84

COMMON NOCTURNE (*Nocturne Vulgaire*)   86

MARINE (*Marine*)   90

WINTER FÊTE (*Fête d'Hiver*)   92

ANGUISH (*Angoisse*)   94

METROPOLITAN (*Métropolitain*)   96

BARBARIAN (*Barbare*)   100

PROMONTORY (*Promontoire*)   104

SCENES (*Scènes*)   108

HISTORIC EVENING (*Soir Historique*)   112

MOTION (*Mouvement*)   116

BOTTOM (*Bottom*)   120

H (*H*)   122

DEVOTIONS (*Dévotion*)   124

DEMOCRACY (*Démocratie*)   128

FAIRY (*Fairy*)   130

WAR (*Guerre*)   132

GENIE (*Génie*)   134

YOUTH (*Jeunesse*)   140

SALE (*Solde*)   146

OTHER PROSE POEMS

THE DESERTS OF LOVE (*Les Déserts de l'Amour*)   152

THREE GOSPEL MORALITIES (*Trois Méditations Johanniques*)   162

Notes on Some Corrections and Revisions   170

A Rimbaud Chronology   175

vi

ILLUMINATIONS

Since the original New Directions publication of *Illuminations* (1946), Rimbaud's manuscripts have been made available to some French scholars. Two editions have resulted: Henri de Bouillane de Lacoste's *Illuminations, Edition Critique* (Mercure de France, 1949), and the Pléiade edition, *Rimbaud, Œuvres Complètes* (Gallimard, 1946), edited by Rolland de Renéville and Jules Mouquet. Now, with the errors of former editors corrected, we probably have the poems as Rimbaud left them. In revising my translation I have consulted both the *Pléiade* and de Lacoste's *Edition Critique*.

The French text I originally used was that of Paterne Berrichon's 1912 edition of *Œuvres de Rim-*

baud, in the 1924 printing (Mercure de France),
which was the standard edition for many years. It
contains Paul Claudel's famous preface, a pious amen
to Isabelle Rimbaud's sanctification of her brother,
in which he calls Rimbaud "a mystic in the savage
state."

The history of the peregrinations of the manu-
script of *Illuminations,* like everything to do with
Rimbaud, is still a matter of dispute among the special-
ists. Most of our information comes from Verlaine,
who certainly knew more about Rimbaud than any one
else, but whose native deviousness and inability to say
anything simply and clearly make most of his state-
ments subject to interpretation, and the interpreta-
tions have confused the confusion. It seems at least
more than probable that in 1875 Rimbaud gave the
manuscript to Verlaine when, after being released
from prison, he pursued his former "companion in
hell" to Stuttgart in a futile attempt to renew their
friendship. It is also more likely than not that it was
the same manuscript which Verlaine (mentioning
simply "prose poems") says, in a letter written
shortly after his visit to Stuttgart, that he had im-
mediately sent, at Rimbaud's request, to Germain
Nouveau in Brussels. How the poems later came into
the possession of Charles de Sivry, Verlaine's brother-
in-law, is still a mystery. After that they passed

through several hands before being published for the first time in five issues of a Symbolist periodical, *La Vogue,* in 1886. That same year *La Vogue* brought them out in book form. Then Félix Fénéon, who had been entrusted with preparing the manuscript for publication, returned it to the publisher, Gustave Kahn. Instead of sending it to Verlaine, who had long been claiming it, Kahn, after holding it for some time, at last, unfortunately, let it be dispersed, giving or selling it here and there. Today, with the exception of the autographs of *Democracie, Devotion* and *Genie,* which have been lost or are still in hiding, the manuscript is divided among several collectors, the bulk of it (thirty-four poems) being in the Lucien-Graux collection.

As for the original order of the poems, Bouillane de Lacoste, after exchanging many letters with Félix Fénéon on the subject, came to the conclusion that, except where two or three poems are written on the same page, there is no way of determining the order assigned them by Rimbaud. After half a century it is hardly surprising that there were lacunae in Fénéon's memories. He describes the manuscript as "a sheaf of loose, unnumbered sheets" of ruled paper, like the paper in schoolboy copybooks (now they are handsomely bound in red morocco!). He cannot remember if the present pagination is his or not, or

whether the poems in the periodical *La Vogue* were brought out in the order they were in when he received the manuscript. But since the manuscript had been handled by many persons after Rimbaud parted with it in Stuttgart, even that order may not have been his. For this edition I have adopted the same order as the Pléiade which, for the first thirty-seven poems, is the same as that in which they first appeared. These are followed by five which were not discovered until later and were published by Vanier in 1895. Considering the unrelated nature of the poems (do I hear voices raised in protest?) the whole question seems rather academic and unimportant. This order is at least preferable to that of Berrichon which I followed before. Berrichon, not having seen the manuscript, could not respect even the sequence of the poems written on the same page, which the present order preserves.

It is again through Verlaine and Verlaine alone that we know Rimbaud's title. The word "Illuminations" does appear once in the manuscript at the end of *Promontoire* between parentheses, but *not*, the experts say, in Rimbaud's handwriting. Although the work has always been called *Les Illuminations* by successive editors and critics (with the exception of de Lacoste), the first time Verlaine mentions it, in a letter to his brother-in-law, Charles de Sivry, in

1878, he calls it simply *Illuminations:* "Have re-read *Illuminations* (painted plates). . . ." Writing at a later period he explains that "the word is English and means *gravures coloriées,* colored plates." That, he says, was the subtitle Rimbaud intended to give his work. To many exegetes it is a kind of sacrilege to suggest that the title could mean anything so simple as colored prints. Verlaine did not understand Rimbaud anyway, they say, and they could even point out that Rimbaud said so himself. In *Une Saison en Enfer (Delire I)*, he has the Foolish Virgin (Verlaine) lament: "I was sure of never entering his world. . . . Sometimes chagrined and sad I said to him, I understand you. He would shrug his shoulders." On the other hand *gravures coloriées* inevitably recalls Rimbaud's *enluminures coloriées,* the brightly colored cheap popular prints or *"images d'Epinal"* of the period, which he lists in *Alchemie du Verbe* among the things that delighted him at the time when he "held in derision the celebrities of modern painting and poetry." But "colored plates," or prints, would be a most misleading subtitle if, as some critics suggest, *Illuminations* means *enluminures* in the sense of medieval illuminated parchments, which were hand colored and not *gravures.* Or if, as the saint-seer-angel-God cults must perforce believe, Rimbaud intended *Illuminations* to be taken in the figura-

tive sense, philosophic or religious—the sudden en-
lightenment of the mind or spirit, either by abstract
wisdom or God (the same in both French and Eng-
lish)—he did not tell the Foolish Virgin. *Genie,*
for one, hardly suggests a *gravure coloriée,* nor do
those poems which were Surrealist before the word
was invented or became a movement. Here the
temptation to quote Shakespeare is almost irresistible.
For, after all, what matters is that the poems do lift
the spirit and dazzle the mind, besides quickening
all the senses. In any case, since we must necessarily
use the title vouched for by Verlaine, I think it
should stand as he first recalled it before time and
alcohol muddled his memory. I have therefore, fol-
lowing de Lacoste, dropped the too definite article,
without, I might add, also adopting as he does, Ver-
laine's too definite, too uncertain, and too odd sub-
title, "painted plates."

The two poems *Marine* and *Movement,* which
now take their place among the *Illuminations,* were
formerly classified as late verse poems. They are not
in the form of any of the other *Illuminations,* are
not strictly speaking prose poems but *vers libres.*
However, the fact that *Marine* was written on the
same page as *Fête d'Hiver* justifies its reclassification.
In the case of *Movement* the reason is less obvious,

except that it is not rhymed. Until recently the late verse poems were included under the general title *Illuminations*. Berrichon gave subtitles: I. *Vers Nouveaux et Chansons;* II. *Poèmes en Prose*. Now scholars agree that the manuscript of *Illuminations* contained only prose poems. For once they are willing to believe Verlaine, who in *Les Poètes Maudits* wrote: "He roamed all the continents, all the oceans after writing, still in prose, a series of superb fragments, the *Illuminations*." And this brings us to the controversial question of whether these poems, "still in prose" (Verlaine says Rimbaud wrote no verse after 1872), were all written before *Une Saison en Enfer,* or after, or some before, some after.

In spite of Verlaine's categorical statement in his preface to the first edition, that the book "was written from 1873 to 1875 in Belgium as well as in England and throughout Germany," sixty-eight years later Enid Starkie, the eminent English scholar and one of the foremost Rimbaud detectives, can speak of the question of the dating of *Illuminations* as "the burning Rimbaud problem today." This is because Rimbaud's first hagiographer, Paterne Berrichon, who was also posthumously his brother-in-law, and Ernest Delahaye, his boyhood friend, in their 1898 edition of Rimbaud's works, gave as their opinion that "a comparison of *Illuminations* and *A Season in Hell*

disproves the dates assigned them by Verlaine. . . ."
They concluded that all the *Illuminations* were writ-
ten before *Une Saison en Enfer* (dated April—
August, 1873, by the poet himself). For Berrichon's
canonizing purposes *A Season in Hell* served ad-
mirably as a proof of Rimbaud's final repudiation of
his past and a sign of grace. It was more appropriate
than *Illuminations* as a swan song for a saint. Ever
since then biographers and exegetes have preferred
the testimony of Berrichon and Delahaye to that of
Verlaine, and the cardinal tenet of the *Rimbaldien*
cult has been that *Une Saison en Enfer* was the
nineteen-year-old boy's farewell to literature, his
mea culpa. For years, moreover, Isabelle's story of
how her brother burned the entire edition of the
work he had himself had printed, provided apodicti-
cal evidence until the "holocaust" legend had re-
gretfully to be abandoned. The edition (five hundred
copies) turned up intact at the printer's in Brussels.
Before that the only copies in existence, the six au-
thor's copies Rimbaud had himself distributed, were
priceless collectors' items. Plenty of fire however was
left in the poem itself, and the farewell-to-literature
theme, with endless variations, persisted. Then came
de Lacoste's *Rimbaud et le Problème des Illumina-
tions,* purporting to prove, by a comparative study
of the *Illuminations* manuscript and dated Rimbaud

autographs, that all the *Illuminations* were written
after the *Season*. If he were right, it would make
nonsense of much Rimbaud exegesis and deflate some
fine *Rimbaldien* prose. Although de Lacoste gives
other reasons for his conviction, his main argument
is graphological. What seemed to clinch the matter
was his interesting discovery that some, or at least
parts of some of the poems, were in the handwriting
of Germain Nouveau, with whom Rimbaud had
lived for a while in London in 1874, and whom he
had not met until late the previous year, *after* the
Season had been written and printed. The farewell-
to-literature exponents were by no means routed by
de Lacoste's triumphant book. His graphological
proof, they were quick to point out, was no proof
at all for, the manuscripts being copies as they con-
vincingly demonstrated, Rimbaud could have written
the poems at any previous date. Since then, eminent
sleuths on both sides have been searching for new
evidence—biographical, psychological or mystical,
and are digging deeper into the poems themselves
for buried relics in vocabulary, syntax, themes, mood,
etc., which, like scattered bones, when assembled
will prove the date of the body. That the poems
may have been written some before, some after, is
also an acceptable theory to many, and has the merit
of not conflicting with the known facts in the case.

No one who has read *Une Saison en Enfer* will, I am sure, deny that it is a *"mea culpa"*—a heartbreaking confession, not of faith, but of failure. One might call it a sort of New Year's resolution which in the end Rimbaud actually kept. He did not, however, say farewell to literature as one waves a handkerchief at a departing ship or train or plane. That theory, the facts disprove. More poet still than penitent, he rushed his confession to the printer. His intense ambition to be a man of letters, his passionate will to be a poet had not been completely consumed in the hell fires of his disgust and despair. In 1874, after the catharsis of *Une Saison en Enfer,* with his new companion in London, he was still interested enough in his own literature to copy the forty-two poems we know as *Illuminations*—even perhaps to write some of them. In 1875, although "in the grip of acute 'philomathic' fever" (languages were to be the open sesame to his new world, escape from the old), the writer's urge to be printed had not left him. Verlaine, in a letter (already mentioned) to Ernest Delahaye, dated May 1, 1875, wrote in his usual ambiguous way: "Rimbaud having asked me to send, to have printed, some prose poems, his, (which I had) to the same Nouveau, then in Brussels (I'm speaking of two months ago) I did send—postage 2 francs 75!!!—instanter. . . ."

Whatever the outcome of the battle of the scholars, we ought to be grateful to de Lacoste for having at least taken a little air out of the mystical balloon of Rimbaud criticism. We may now be permitted to read Rimbaud without praying. Etiemble in his prodigious de-mythefying thesis, *Le Mythe de Rimbaud,* says that if he had to write a life of Rimbaud he would be "incapable of forming a single sentence" so suspect do all the facts still seem to him. A pity— for a brief (necessarily if only factual) unbiased biography would be a refreshing start toward a fresh approach to his work. Etiemble's concluding advice is best: *"Revenir au texte."* I often wish, when I read some of Rimbaud's exegetes, that Rimbaud had taken as an epigraph for his *Illuminations* Aloysius Bertrand's injunction: "Here is my book as I wrote it and as it should be read before the commentators obscure it with their elucidations."

English readers who are interested to know more about the "burning problem" will find the arguments briefly reviewed by that erudite and perceptive authority on French literature, Wallace Fowlie, in his *Rimbaud's Illuminations.* For a bird's-eye view of a hundred years of Rimbaud and *Rimbaldiens* (anti-*Rimbaldiens* too) I recommend Enid Starkie's Zaharoff Lecture for 1954: *Rimbaud, 1854–1954* (Ox-

ford University Press). It is an excellent summary
of the history of Rimbaud's literary output and the
far more abundant output of his critics and biogra-
phers.

*   *   *

Revised Translation of *Illuminations*

To revise, the dictionary says, is to correct, to
improve, to bring up to date. Corrected and brought
up to date to conform to the latest scholarly findings,
my translation, I hope, is also improved. When a
translation of poetry like Rimbaud's is whisked out
of the translator's head, so to speak, into the hands
of the printer, the very excess of the translator's en-
thusiasm mitigates his critical acumen, which needs
a cooler climate. Ideally, a translation of poetry as
mysteriously beautiful as Rimbaud's last works should
be kept for months—years—before being published.
On the other hand, nothing reveals a translation's
mistakes, inadequacies and infelicities with such ruth-
lessness as the printed page.

The difficulty in translating the *Illuminations* is
not, as many people seem to think, their obscurity.
It is their extreme density combined with their pris-
matic and protean quality. In most of them the

xviii

literal meaning, which has been lost in the many-faceted poetic meaning, is scarcely more important than a composer's initial idea which becomes completely metamorphosed into music. By his special use of language Rimbaud's thought becomes condensed into nothing but poetry. And this dense poetic mass is continually moving and changing. One is reminded of a chemical process/ as words join other words in the sentences to form an ever more complex compound. And who can tell, of these kaleidoscopic atoms, which ones are ideas and which ones are objects? To *activate* English words to perform similar miracles—that is the difficulty.

It is not to excuse any failures on my part that I point out the difficulties, but to warn the English reader that his imagination must be ready to make up for my deficiencies.

As this revised translation of *Illuminations* goes to press, there is that same old sensation in the pit of my stomach—the dreadful anticipation of the revelations of the printed page. Once more, I have to remind myself of what Valéry said of writers (substituting "translation" for "work"): "One does not finish a [translation], one abandons it."

* * *

Rimbaud's Other Prose Poems

The Deserts of Love and *Gospel Moralities* (both probably fragmentary series) have been incorporated in this edition of *Illuminations* in order to complete the publication in English of all Rimbaud's prose poems—at least all that have so far come to light. *A Season in Hell* appears in a separate volume in New Directions' *New Classics* series. That Rimbaud wrote other prose poems we know from references to them by both Verlaine and Delahaye, so that we may still hope that some of them will one day turn up as did two of the Biblical poems only a short time ago. I should particularly like to see the one of which Verlaine said that it "contained strange mysticities and the keenest psychological insights"— probably the famous lost *Chasse Spirituelle* which probably no one but Verlaine ever saw.

We are told by Delahaye that *Les Deserts de l'Amour* was Rimbaud's first prose poem, that it was written in the spring of 1871, and that the idea of attempting this poetic form came to him after reading Baudelaire's prose poems. If *Les Deserts de l'Amour* was really modeled on *Spleen de Paris*, one can only say that it is as "singularly different" as Baudelaire said his work was from its "mysterious

and brilliant model," *Gaspard de la Nuit*. The spark
could have come from a single line in Baudelaire's
dedication to Arsène Houssaye: "Which one of us,
in our ambitious moments, has not dreamed of the
miracle of a poetic prose, musical without rhyme
and without rhythm, supple enough and abrupt
enough to adapt itself to the lyrical movements of
the soul, the undulations of revery, the jolts of con-
science." Too many of the *Petits Poèmes en Prose*
are only prose, even prosaic, whereas *The Deserts of
Love* is pure poetry. At least to me. Not, it would
seem, to most Rimbaud commentators, since they
have strangely neglected it. Enid Starkie even pre-
sents it as merely a "psychological study" whose
"interest does not lie in its literary value." De Lacoste
calls it "one long sob of a disenchanted child"—but
a child, I should say, who sobs with the art of a
conscious craftsman. The poem was first published
in 1906. Berrichon dated its composition as "prob-
ably" late 1871. De Lacoste gives 1872 as the date
of the manuscript, which is again quite evidently a
copy.

No title appears in the manuscript of the three
poems which, for reference convenience and with a
bow to Jules Laforgue, I have called *Gospel Morali-
ties*. The first two are a recent discovery, and this is

the first time they have been translated into English
and published in this country. They were found,
after the death of Mme. Léon Vanier, stuck at the
back of a drawer containing other manuscripts be-
longing to her late husband, Verlaine's publisher, and
were acquired by H. Matarasso. Presented by Mata-
rasso and Bouillane de Lacoste, they were published
in the *Mercure de France,* January, 1948, with a
detailed description of the manuscript. It was a
doubly precious find for, on the reverse side of the
single sheet of paper on which they were written, is
a rough draft of a part of *Une Saison en Enfer.* The
beginning of the first poem is apparently still miss-
ing. The use of the pronoun instead of Jesus' name
in the first line indicates that he has already been
mentioned. It seems probable that the poem began
with the scene at Jacob's well and must at least have
included the woman's words: "Sir, I perceive that
you are a prophet." Perhaps some day the other page
will also turn up, perhaps even other poems of the
same series, perhaps a title. . . .

De Lacoste calls the three poems: *A Samaria, En
Galilée, Beth-Saïda* (better known as "Bethesda").
The last of these, first published in 1897, was also
written on one side of a rough draft of another
fragment of the *Season,* called *Fausse Confession*

(False Confession), which Rimbaud later changed to *Nuit de l'Enfer* (Night of Hell). Berrichon, at a loss to classify it, published it at different times either at the end of *Illuminations* or at the beginning of *Une Saison en Enfer,* thinking that Rimbaud might have intended it as a prologue, afterwards discarding it for the one he published. With the discovery of the two other poems taken from the Gospel of St. John, it becomes clear that it was one of the same biblical series. Four words, long a mystery, at the top of the *Beth-Saïda* autograph, *"demandant grâce au jour,"* are found to be the end of the lovely last line of *In Galilee.* Their position serves to establish the order of the poems. They were written some time in 1873, the same year as *Une Saison en Enfer,* as indicated by the similarity of the handwriting on the rough drafts. Like the *Season,* they were probably written at his mother's farm at Roche. They suggest a Bible at hand, which in turn suggests the house of *"la mother"* rather than the room in London shared by the *"drôle de ménage."*

Jules Laforgue, who with his gift for subtle accuracy called Rimbaud "the only isomer of Baudelaire," is generally thought to be the originator of this kind of ironic distortion of legend. These poems show Rimbaud as his precursor. The manuscripts

having been found among Léon Vanier's papers tempts one to wonder if it is not significant that Vanier was Verlaine's publisher, as well as Laforgue's.

BY WAY OF A PREFACE

The following letters form a natural preface to the Illuminations *in which Rimbaud put into practice the poetic theory here tentatively described. The poems enclosed in the letters are not examples of his new doctrine. They are still in the old form. Not until the* Illuminations *did Rimbaud find the "new forms that inventions of the unknown demand." Perhaps in them he has not revealed to us "the unknown"; perhaps he did not succeed in being a visionary in his occult sense. But he succeeded: he invented new forms, a new language, and he has made us smell and hear and see perfumes, sounds, colors of an unknown of his invention.*

LETTER TO GEORGE IZAMBARD
(DOUAI)

Charleville, May 13, 1871

Dear Sir:

So you are a teacher again! One's duty is to Society, as you have told me; you are a member of the teaching body: you're running in the right track. I too, I follow the principle: I am cynically getting myself kept. I unearth old imbeciles from our school: the stupidest, rottenest, meanest things I can think of—in action or words—I serve up to them: I'm paid in steins and ponies. *Stat mater dolorosa, dum pendet filius.* My duty is to Society, it's true,—and I'm right. You too, you're right, for today. As a matter of fact all you see in your principle is subjective poetry: your obstinacy in going back to the pedagogic trough—pardon me—proves it. But you'll just end up self-satisfied without having done anything, not having wanted to do anything. Not to menton that your subjective poetry will always be horribly insipid. Some day I hope—many others hope so too—I'll see objective poetry in your principle. I shall see it more sincerely than you will do it! I'll be a worker: that is the idea that holds me back when mad rage

drives me toward the battle of Paris where so many workers are still dying while I write to you! As for my working now, never, never; I'm on strike.

Now I am going in for debauch. Why? I want to be a poet, and I am working to make myself a *visionary:* you won't possibly understand, and I don't know how to explain it to you. To arrive at the unknown through the disordering of *all the senses,* that's the point. The sufferings will be tremendous, but one must be strong, be born a poet: it is in no way my fault. It is wrong to say: I think. One should say: I am thought. Pardon the pun.*

I is some one else. So much the worse for the wood that discovers it's a violin, and to hell with the heedless who cavil about something they know nothing about!

You're not a teacher for me. I offer you the following: is it satire, as you would say? Is it poetry? At any rate it's fantasy. But I beg you, please don't underscore it, not with pencil or too much with thought either:

Poem enclosed: *The Tortured Heart (Le Coeur Supplicié).*

* "Allusion, according to G. Izambard, to an historic pun. When Voltaire came back from England, Louis XV is said to have asked him: 'What did you learn over there?' 'To think, Sire' (*penser,* to think) 'Horses?' (*panser,* to groom horses)"

 J.-M. Carré, *Lettres de la Vie Littéraire d'Arthur Rimbaud.*

This does not mean nothing.—Answer: % M. Deverrièrre, for A.R.

Affectionate greetings,
Arthur Rimbaud.

Letter to Paul Demeny
(DOUAI)

Charleville, May 15, 1871

I have decided to give you an hour of new literature. I begin at once with a psalm of current interest.

Poem enclosed: *Paris War Song (Chant de Guerre Parisien)*.

And now follows a discourse on the future of poetry:—

All ancient poetry culminated in Greek poetry, harmonious Life. From Greece to the Romantic movement—Middle Ages—there are men of letters, versifiers. From Ennius to Theroldus, from Theroldus to Casimir Delavigne, nothing but rhymed prose, a game, fatty degeneration and glory of countless idiotic generations: Racine is the pure, the strong, the great man. Had his rhymes been effaced, his hemistitches got mixed up, today the Divine Imbecile would be as unknown as any old author of

Origins. After Racine the game gets moldy. It lasted for two thousand years!

Neither a joke, nor a paradox. Reason inspires me with more certainties on this subject than any *Young-France* ever had angers. Besides, newcomers have a right to condemn their ancestors: one is at home and there's plenty of time.

Romanticism has never been properly judged. Who was there to judge it? The critics!! The Romantics? who prove so clearly that the song is very seldom the work, that is, the idea sung and understood by the singer.

For, I is some one else. If brass wakes up a trumpet, it isn't to blame. To me this is evident: I witness the birth of my thought: I look at it, I listen to it: I give a stroke of the bow: the symphony begins to stir in the depths or comes bursting onto the stage.

If the old fools had not hit upon the false significance of the Ego only, we should not now have to sweep away these millions of skeletons who, since time immemorial, have been accumulating the products of those cockeyed intellects claiming themselves to be the authors.

In Greece, I have said, verses and lyres, rhythms: Action. After that, music and rhymes are games, pasttimes. The study of this past charms the curi-

ous: many delight in reviving these antiquities:—
the pleasure is theirs.

Universal Mind has always thrown out its ideas
naturally; men would pick up part of these fruits
of the brain; they acted through, wrote books with
them: and so things went along, since man did not
work on himself, not being yet awake, or not yet in
the fullness of his dream. Writers were functionaries.
Author, creator, poet,—that man has never existed!

The first study for a man who wants to be a poet
is the knowledge of himself, entire. He searches his
soul, he inspects it, he tests it, he learns it. As soon
as he knows it, he cultivates it: it seems simple: in
every brain a natural development is accomplished:
so many egoists proclaim themselves authors; others
attribute their intellectual progress to themselves!
But the soul has to be made monstrous, that's the
point:—like *comprachicos,* if you like! Imagine a
man planting and cultivating warts on his face.

One must, I say, be a *visionary,* make oneself a
visionary.

The poet makes himself a *visionary* through a
long, a prodigious and rational disordering of *all* the
senses. Every form of love, of suffering, of madness;
he searches himself, he consumes all the poisons in
him, keeping only their quintessences. Ineffable tor-
ture in which he will need all his faith and super-

human strength, the great criminal, the great sick-man, the accursed,—and the supreme Savant! For he arrives at the unknown! Since he has cultivated his soul—richer to begin with than any other! He arrives at the unknown: and even if, half crazed, in the end, he loses the understanding of his visions, he has seen them! Let him be destroyed in his leap by those unnamable, unutterable and innumerable things: there will come other horrible workers: they will begin at the horizons where he has succumbed.

—continued in six minutes—

Here, I interpolate a second psalm outside the text: kindly lend a friendly ear and everybody will be charmed. I hold the bow in my hand, I begin:

Poem enclosed, *My Little Sweethearts* (*Mes Petites Amoureuses*).

That's that. And if I weren't afraid of making you spend over 60 centimes for postage—I poor waif * without a red cent to my name for the last seven months!—I would offer you my *Paris Lovers* (*Amants de Paris*), one hundred hexameters, dear Sir, and my *Death of Paris* (*Mort de Paris*),** two hundred hexameters!

—I continue—

So then, the poet is truly a thief of fire.

* Rimbaud's poem, *Les Effarés* (*The Waifs*), describing haggard street urchins gazing through a cellar vent at bread in a baker's oven.

** These two poems have not been found.

Humanity is his responsibility, even the animals; he must see to it that his inventions can be smelled, felt, heard. If what he brings back from beyond has form, he gives it form, if it is formless, he gives it formlessness. A language must be found; as a matter of fact, all speech being an idea, the time of a universal language will come! One has to be an academician —deader than a fossil—to finish a dictionary of any language at all. The weak-minded, beginning with the first letter of the alphabet, would soon be raving mad!

This harangue would be of the soul for the soul, summing up everything, perfumes, sounds, colors, thought grappling thought, and pulling. The poet would define the amount of unknown arising in his time in the universal soul; he would give more than the formula of his thought, more than the annotation of his march toward Progress! Enormity become norm, absorbed by every one, he would truly be the multiplier of progress!

This future, as you see, will be materialistic. Always full of *Number* and *Harmony*, these poems would be made to last. As a matter of fact it will still be Greek poetry in a way.

This eternal art will have its functions since poets are citizens. Poetry will no longer accompany action but will lead it.

These poets are going to exist! When the infinite servitude of woman shall have ended, when she will be able to live by and for herself; then, man—hitherto abominable—having given her her freedom, she too will be a poet. Woman will discover the unknown. Will her world be different from ours? She will discover strange, unfathomable things, repulsive, delicious. We shall take them, we shall understand them.

Meantime ask the poet for the new—ideas and forms. All the bright boys will imagine they have satisfied this demand: it isn't that at all!

The first Romantics were *visionaries* without quite realizing it: the cultivation of their souls began accidently: abandoned locomotives, still burning, that go on running along the rails for awhile. Lamartine is at times a *visionary,* but strangled by the old form. Hugo, too much of a ham, has really vision in his last works: *Les Misérables* is a true poem. I have *Les Chatiments* at hand; Stella shows the limit of Hugo's visionary powers. Too much Belmontet and Lamennais, too many Jehovahs and columns, old, dead enormities.

Musset is fourteen times execrable for us, suffering generations carried away by visions—to whom his angel's sloth is an insult! Oh! the insipid *Tales* and *Proverbs!* O the *Nights!* O *Rolla,* O *Namouna!* O the *Chalice!* It's all so French, that is, detestable to

the last degree; French, not Parisian! Again the work of the evil genius that inspired Rabelais, Voltaire, Jean La Fontaine with commentary by Mr. Taine! Spring-like, de Musset's wit! Charming, his love! Regular enamel painting, solid poetry! French poetry will long be enjoyed—but in France. Every grocer-boy can reel off a Rollaesque apostrophe, every budding priest has the five hundred rhymes hidden away in a secret note-book. At fifteen these flights of passion make boys ruttish; at sixteen they are already satisfied to recite them with feeling; at eighteen, even seventeen, every schoolboy who has the chance, acts like Rolla, writes a Rolla! Perhaps some may still even die of it. Musset achieved nothing. There were visions behind the gauze curtains; he closed his eyes. Dragged from café to school-room, French and driveling, the fine corpse is dead, and from now on, let's not even take the trouble to wake him with our execrations!

The second Romantics are really visionaries: Théophile Gautier, Leconte de Lisle, Théodore de Banville. But, inspecting the invisible and hearing the unheard being entirely different from recapturing the spirit of dead things, Baudelaire is the first visionary, king of poets, a *real God!* Unfortunately he lived in too artistic a milieu; and his much vaunted style is

trivial. Inventions of the unknown demand new forms.

Trained in the old forms: among the simpletons, A. Renaud,—has done his Rolla; L. Grandet,—has done his Rolla; the *Gaulois* and the Mussets, G. Lafenestre, Coran, C.-L. Popelin, Soulary, L. Salles; the schoolboys, Marc, Aicard, Theuriet; the dead and the imbeciles, Antran, Barbier, L. Pichat, Lemoyne; the Deschamps, the des Essarts; the Bohemians; the women; the talents, Leon Dierx and Sully Prudhomme, Coppée.—The new school, called Parnassian, has two visionaries, Albert Merat and Paul Verlaine, a true poet. And there you are.

So I am working to make myself a *visionary*.

—And now let us close with a pious chant.

Poem enclosed, *Squattings* (*Accroupissements*).

You will be damnable if you don't answer: quickly, for in a week I shall be in Paris perhaps.

Goodbye.

A. Rimbaud

ILLUMINATIONS

APRÈS LE DÉLUGE

Aussitôt que l'idée du Déluge se fut rassise,

Un lièvre s'arrêta dans les sainfoins et les clochettes mouvantes, et dit sa prière à l'arc-en-ciel, à travers la toile de l'araignée.

Oh! les pierres précieuses qui se cachaient,—les fleurs qui regardaient déjà.

Dans la grande rue sale, les étals se dressèrent, et l'on tira les barques vers la mer étagée là-haut comme sur les gravures.

Le sang coula, chez Barbe-Bleue,—aux abattoirs, dans les cirques, où le sceau de Dieu blêmit les fenêtres. Le sang et le lait coulèrent.

Les castors bâtirent. Les "mazagrans" fumèrent dans les estaminets.

Dans la grande maison de vitres encore ruisselante, les enfants en deuil regardèrent les merveilleuses images.

AFTER THE DELUGE

As SOON as the idea of the Deluge had subsided,

A hare stopped in the clover and swaying flower-bells, and said a prayer to the rainbow, through the spider's web.

Oh! the precious stones that began to hide,—and the flowers that already looked around.

In the dirty main street, stalls were set up and boats were hauled toward the sea, high tiered as in old prints.

Blood flowed at Blue Beard's,—through slaughter-houses, in circuses, where the windows were blanched by God's seal. Blood and milk flowed.

Beavers built. "Mazagrans" smoked in the little bars.

In the big glass house, still dripping, children in mourning looked at the marvelous pictures.

Une porte claqua; et, sur la place du hameau, l'enfant tourna ses bras, compris des girouettes et des coqs des clochers de partout, sous l'éclatante giboulée.

Madame * * * établit un piano dans les Alpes. La messe et les premières communions se célébrèrent aux cent mille autels de la cathédrale.

Les caravanes partirent. Et le Splendide-Hôtel fut bâti dans le chaos de glaces et de nuit du pôle.

Depuis lors, la Lune entendit les chacals piaulant par les déserts de thym,—et les églogues en sabots grognant dans le verger. Puis, dans la futaie violette, bourgeonnante, Eucharis me dit que c'était le printemps.

Sourds, étang;—Écume, roule sur le pont et par-dessus les bois;—draps noirs et orgues, éclairs et tonnerre, montez et roulez;—eaux et tristesses, montez et relevez les Déluges.

Car depuis qu'ils se sont dissipés,—oh, les pierres précieuses s'enfouissant, et les fleurs ouvertes!—c'est un ennui! Et la Reine, la Sorcière qui allume sa braise dans le pot de terre, ne voudra jamais nous raconter ce qu'elle sait, et que nous ignorons.

A door banged; and in the village square the little boy waved his arms, understood by weather vanes and cocks on steeples everywhere, in the bursting shower.

Madame*** installed a piano in the Alps. Mass and first communions were celebrated at the hundred thousand altars of the cathedral.

Caravans set out. And Hotel Splendid was built in the chaos of ice and of the polar night.

Ever after the moon heard jackals howling across the deserts of thyme, and eclogues in wooden shoes growling in the orchard. Then in the violet and budding forest, Eucharis told me it was spring.

Gush, pond,—Foam, roll on the bridge and over the woods;—black palls and organs, lightning and thunder, rise and roll;—waters and sorrows rise and launch the Floods again.

For since they have been dissipated—oh! the precious stones being buried and the opened flowers! —it's unbearable! and the Queen, the Witch who lights her fire in the earthen pot will never tell us what she knows, and what we do not know.

5

ENFANCE

Cette idole, yeux noirs et crin jaune, sans parents
ni cour, plus noble que la fable, mexicaine et flamande;
son domaine, azur et verdure insolents, court sur des
plages nommées, par des vagues sans vaisseaux, de
noms férocement grecs, slaves, celtiques.

A la lisière de la forêt,—les fleurs de rêve tintent,
éclatent, éclairent,—la fille à lèvre d'orange, les
genoux croisés dans le clair déluge qui sourd des prés,
nudité qu'ombrent, traversent et habillent les arcs-en-
ciel, la flore, la mer.

Dames qui tournoient sur les terrasses voisines de
la mer; enfantes et géantes, superbes noires dans la
mousse vert-de-gris, bijoux debout sur le sol gras des

CHILDHOOD

I

That idol, black eyes and yellow mop, without
parents or court, nobler than Mexican and Flemish
fables; his domain, insolent azure and verdure, runs
over beaches called by the shipless waves, names
ferociously Greek, Slav, Celt.

At the border of the forest—dream flowers tinkle,
flash, and flare,—the girl with orange lips, knees
crossed in the clear flood that gushes from the fields,
nakedness shaded, traversed, dressed by rainbow,
flora, sea.

Ladies who stroll on terraces adjacent to the sea;
baby girls and giantesses, superb blacks in the ver-
digris moss, jewels upright on the rich ground of

bosquets et des jardinets dégelés,—jeunes mères et grandes sœurs aux regards pleins de pèlerinages, sultanes, princesses de démarche et de costume tyranniques, petites étrangères et personnes doucement malheureuses.

Quel ennui, l'heure du "cher corps" et "cher cœur."

II

C'est elle, la petite morte, derrière les rosiers.—La jeune maman trépassée descend le perron.—La calèche du cousin crie sur le sable.—Le petit frère (il est aux Indes!) là, devant le couchant, sur le pré d'œillets.—Les vieux qu'on a enterrés tout droits dans le rempart aux giroflées.

L'essaim des feuilles d'or entoure la maison du général. Ils sont dans le midi.—On suit la route rouge pour arriver à l'auberge vide. Le château est à vendre; les persiennes sont détachées.—Le curé aura emporté la clef de l'église.—Autour du parc, les loges des gardes sont inhabitées. Les palissades sont si hautes qu'on ne voit que les cimes bruissantes. D'ailleurs, il n'y a rien à voir là-dedans.

groves and little thawed gardens,—young mothers and big sisters with eyes full of pilgrimages, sultanas, princesses tyrannical of costume and carriage, little foreign misses and young ladies gently unhappy.

What boredom, the hour of the "dear body" and "dear heart."

II

It is she, the little girl, dead behind the rosebushes. —The young mamma, deceased, comes down the stoop.—The cousin's carriage creaks on the sand.— The little brother (he is in India!) there, before the western sky in the meadow of pinks. The old men who have been buried upright in the rampart overgrown with gillyflowers.

Swarms of golden leaves surround the general's house. They are in the south.—You follow the red road to reach the empty inn. The château is for sale; the shutters are coming off. The priest must have taken away the key of the church. Around the park the keepers' cottages are uninhabited. The enclosures are so high that nothing can be seen but the rustling tree tops. Besides, there is nothing to be seen within.

9

Les prés remontent aux hameaux sans coqs, sans enclumes. L'écluse est levée. O les Calvaires et les moulins du désert, les îles et les meules!

Des fleurs magiques bourdonnaient. Les talus le berçaient. Des bêtes d'une élégance fabuleuse circulaient. Les nuées s'amassaient sur la haute mer faite d'une éternité de chaudes larmes.

III

Au bois il y a un oiseau, son chant vous arrête et vous fait rougir.

Il y a une horloge qui ne sonne pas.

Il y a une fondrière avec un nid de bêtes blanches.

Il y a une cathédrale qui descend et un lac qui monte.

Il y a une petite voiture abandonnée dans le taillis ou qui descend le sentier en courant, enrubannée.

The meadows go up to the hamlets without anvils or cocks. The sluice gate is open. O the Calvaries and the windmills of the desert, the islands and the haystacks!

Magic flowers droned. The slopes cradled him. Beasts of a fabulous elegance moved about. The clouds gathered over the high sea, formed of an eternity of hot tears.

III

In the woods there is a bird; his song stops you and makes you blush.

There is a clock that never strikes.

There is a hollow with a nest of white beasts.

There is a cathedral that goes down and a lake that goes up.

There is a little carriage abandoned in the copse or that goes running down the road beribboned.

Il y a une troupe de petits comédiens en costumes, aperçus sur la route à travers la lisière du bois.

Il y a enfin, quand l'on a faim et soif, quelqu'un qui vous chasse.

IV

Je suis le saint, en prière sur la terrasse, comme les bêtes pacifiques paissent jusqu'à la mer de Palestine.

Je suis le savant au fauteuil sombre. Les branches et la pluie se jettent à la croisée de la bibliothèque.

Je suis le piéton de la grand'route par les bois nains; la rumeur des écluses couvre mes pas. Je vois long-temps la mélancolique lessive d'or du couchant.

Je serais bien l'enfant abandonné sur la jetée partie à la haute mer, le petit valet suivant l'allée dont le front touche le ciel.

Les sentiers sont âpres. Les monticules se couvrent de genêts. L'air est immobile. Que les oiseaux et les sources sont loin! Ce ne peut être que la fin du monde, en avançant.

There is a troupe of little actors in costume, glimpsed on the road through the border of the woods.

And then, when you are hungry and thirsty, there is someone who drives you away.

IV

I am the saint at prayer on the terrace like the peaceful beasts that graze down to the sea of Palestine.

I am the scholar of the dark armchair. Branches and rain hurl themselves at the windows of my library.

I am the pedestrian of the highroad by way of the dwarf woods; the roar of the sluices drowns my steps. I can see for a long time the melancholy wash of the setting sun.

I might well be the child abandoned on the jetty on its way to the high seas, the little farm boy following the lane, its forehead touching the sky.

The paths are rough. The hillocks are covered with broom. The air is motionless. How far away are the birds and the springs! It can only be the end of the world ahead.

13

V

Qu'on me loue enfin ce tombeau, blanchi à la chaux avec les lignes du ciment en relief,—très loin sous terre.

Je m'accoude à la table, la lampe éclaire très vivement ces journaux que je suis idiot de relire, ces livres sans intérêt.

A une distance énorme au-dessus de mon salon souterrain, les maisons s'implantent, les brumes s'assemblent. La boue est rouge ou noire. Ville monstrueuse, nuit sans fin!

Moins haut, sont des égouts. Aux côtés, rien que l'épaisseur du globe. Peut-être les gouffres d'azur, des puits de feu. C'est peut-être sur ces plans que se rencontrent lunes et comètes, mers et fables.

Aux heures d'amertume, je m'imagine des boules de saphir, de métal. Je suis maître du silence. Pourquoi une apparence de soupirail blêmirait-elle au coin de la voûte?

ILLUMINATIONS

V

Let them rent me this whitewashed tomb, at last, with cement lines in relief,—far down under ground.

I lean my elbows on the table, the lamp shines brightly on these newspapers I am fool enough to read again, these stupid books.

At an enormous distance above my subterranean parlor, houses take root, fogs gather. The mud is red or black. Monstrous city, night without end!

Less high are the sewers. At the sides, nothing but the thickness of the globe. Chasms of azure, wells of fire perhaps. Perhaps it is on these levels that moons and comets meet, fables and seas.

In hours of bitterness, I imagine balls of sapphire, of metal. I am master of silence. Why should the semblance of an opening pale under one corner of the vault?

CONTE

Un Prince était vexé de ne s'être employé jamais qu'à la perfection des générosités vulgaires. Il prévoyait d'étonnantes révolutions de l'amour, et soupçonnait ses femmes de pouvoir mieux que cette complaisance agrémentée de ciel et de luxe. Il voulait voir la vérité, l'heure du désir et de la satisfaction essentiels. Que ce fût ou non une aberration de piété, il voulut. Il possédait au moins un assez large pouvoir humain.

Toutes les femmes qui l'avaient connu furent assassinées: quel saccage du jardin de la beauté! Sous le sabre, elles le bénirent. Il n'en commanda point de nouvelles.—Les femmes réapparurent.

Il tua tous ceux qui le suivaient, après la chasse ou les libations.—Tous le suivaient.

Il s'amusa à égorger les bêtes de luxe. Il fit flamber les palais. Il se ruait sur les gens et les taillait en pièces.

TALE

A Prince was vexed at having devoted himself only to the perfection of ordinary generosities. He foresaw astonishing revolutions of love and suspected his women of being able to do better than their habitual acquiescence embellished by heaven and luxury. He wanted to see the truth, the hour of essential desire and gratification. Whether this was an aberration of piety or not, that is what he wanted. Enough worldly power, at least, he had.

All the women who had known him were assassinated; what havoc in the garden of beauty! At the point of the sword they blessed him. He did not order new ones.—The women reappeared.

He killed all those who followed him, after the hunt or the libations.—All followed him.

He amused himself cutting the throats of rare animals. He set palaces on fire. He would rush upon

—La foule, les toits d'or, les belles bêtes existaient encore.

Peut-on s'extasier dans la destruction, se rajeunir par la cruauté! Le peuple ne murmura pas. Personne n'offrit le concours de ses vues.

Un soir, il galopait fièrement. Un Génie apparut, d'une beauté ineffable, inavouable même. De sa physionomie et de son maintien ressortait la promesse d'un amour multiple et complexe! d'un bonheur indicible, insupportable même! Le Prince et le Génie s'anéantirent probablement dans la santé essentielle. Comment n'auraient-ils pas pu en mourir? Ensemble donc ils moururent.

Mais ce Prince décéda, dans son palais, à un âge ordinaire. Le Prince était le Génie. Le Génie était le Prince.—La musique savante manque à notre désir.

people and hack them to pieces.—The throngs, the gilded roofs, the beautiful animals still remained.

Can one be in ecstasies over destruction and by cruelty rejuvenated! The people did not complain. No one offered him the benefit of his views.

One evening he was proudly galloping. A Genie appeared, of ineffable beauty, unavowable even. In his face and in his bearing shone the promise of a complex and multiple love! of an indescribable happiness, unendurable even. The Prince and the Genie annihilated each other probably in essential health. How could they have helped dying of it? Together then they died.

But this Prince died in his palace at an ordinary age, the Prince was the Genie, the Genie was the Prince.—There is no sovereign music for our desire.

PARADE

Des drôles très solides. Plusieurs ont exploité vos mondes. Sans besoins, et peu pressés de mettre en œuvre leurs brillantes facultés et leur expérience de vos consciences. Quels hommes mûrs! Des yeux hébétés à la façon de la nuit d'été, rouges et noirs, tricolorés, d'acier piqué d'étoiles d'or; des facies déformés, plombés, blêmis, incendiés; des enrouements folâtres! La démarche cruelle des oripeaux!—Il y a quelques jeunes,—comment regarderaient-ils Chérubin? —pourvus de voix effrayantes et de quelques ressources dangereuses. On les envoie prendre du dos en ville, affublés d'un *luxe* dégoûtant.

O le plus violent Paradis de la grimace enragée! Pas de comparaison avec vos Fakirs et les autres bouffonneries scéniques. Dans des costumes improvisés, avec le goût du mauvais rêve, ils jouent des complaintes, des tragédies de malandrins et de demi-

SIDE SHOW

Very sturdy rogues. Several have exploited your worlds. With no needs, and in no hurry to make use of their brilliant faculties and their knowledge of your consciences. What ripe men! Eyes vacant like the summer night, red and black, tricolored, steel studded with gold stars; faces distorted, leaden, blanched, ablaze; burlesque hoarsenesses! The cruel strut of flashy finery! Some are young,—how would they look on Cherubin?—endowed with terrifying voices and some dangerous resources. They are sent snaring in the town, tricked out with nauseating *luxury*.

O the most violent Paradise of the furious grimace! Not to be compared with your Fakirs and other theatrical buffooneries. In improvised costumes like something out of a bad dream, they enact heroic romances of brigands and of demigods, more spirit-

dieux spirituels comme l'histoire ou les religions ne
l'ont jamais été. Chinois, Hottentots, bohêmiens,
niais, hyènes, Molochs, vieilles démences, démons
sinistres, ils mêlent les tours populaires, maternels,
avec les poses et les tendresses bestiales. Ils interpré-
teraient des pièces nouvelles et des chansons "bonnes
filles". Maîtres jongleurs, ils transforment le lieu et les
personnes et usent de la comédie magnétique. Les
yeux flambent, le sang chante, les os s'élargissent, les
larmes et des filets rouges ruissellent. Leur raillerie ou
leur terreur dure une minute, ou des mois entiers.

J'ai seul la clef de cette parade sauvage.

ing than history or religions have ever been. Chinese, Hottentots, gypsies, simpletons, hyenas, Molochs, old dementias, sinister demons, they combine popular maternal turns with bestial poses and caresses. They would interpret new plays, "romantic" songs. Master jugglers, they transform place and persons and have recourse to magnetic comedy. Eyes flame, blood sings, bones swell, tears and red trickles flow. Their clowning or their terror lasts a minute or entire months.

I alone have the key to this savage side show.

ANTIQUE

Gracieux fils de Pan! Autour de ton front couronné de fleurettes et de baies, tes yeux, des boules précieuses, remuent. Tachées de lie brune, tes joues se creusent. Tes crocs luisent. Ta poitrine ressemble à une cithare, des tintements circulent dans tes bras blonds. Ton cœur bat dans ce ventre où dort le double sexe. Promène-toi, la nuit, en mouvant doucement cette cuisse, cette seconde cuisse et cette jambe de gauche.

ANTIQUE

Gracious son of Pan! Around your forehead crowned with flowerets and with laurel, restlessly roll those precious balls, your eyes. Spotted with brown lees, your cheeks are hollow. Your fangs gleam. Your breast is like a lyre, tinklings circulate through your pale arms. Your heart beats in that belly where sleeps the double sex. Walk through the night, gently moving that thigh, that second thigh, and that left leg.

BEING BEAUTEOUS

Devant une neige, un Être de Beauté de haute taille. Des sifflements de mort et des cercles de musique sourde font monter, s'élargir et trembler comme un spectre ce corps adoré; des blessures écarlates et noires éclatent dans les chairs superbes.—Les couleurs propres de la vie se foncent, dansent, et se dégagent autour de la Vision, sur le chantier.—Et les frissons s'élèvent et grondent, et la saveur forcenée de ces effets se chargeant avec les sifflements mortels et les rauques musiques que le monde, loin derrière nous, lance sur notre mère de beauté,—elle recule, elle se dresse. Oh! nos os sont revêtus d'un nouveau corps amoureux.

O la face cendrée, l'écusson de crin, les bras de cristal! le canon sur lequel je dois m'abattre à travers la mêlée des arbres et de l'air léger!

BEAUTEOUS BEING

Against the snow a Being of high-statured Beauty. Whistlings of death and circles of secret music make the adored body, like a specter, rise, expand, and quiver; wounds of black and scarlet burst in the superb flesh.—Life's own colors darken, dance, and drift around the Vision in the making.—Shudders rise and rumble, and the delirious savor of these effects clashing with the deadly hissings and the hoarse music that the world, far behind us, hurls at our mother of beauty,—she recoils, she rears up. Oh, our bones are clothed with an amorous new body.

O the ashy face, the crined escutcheon, the crystal arms! the cannon on which I am to fall in the melee of trees and of light air!

VIES

I

O les énormes avenues du pays saint, les terrasses du temple! Qu'a-t-on fait du brahmane qui m'expliqua les Proverbes? D'alors, de là-bas, je vois encore même les vieilles! Je me souviens des heures d'argent et de soleil vers les fleuves, la main de la campagne sur mon épaule, et de nos caresses debout dans les plaines poivrées.—Un envol de pigeons écarlates tonne autour de ma pensée.—Exilé ici, j'ai eu une scène où jouer les chefs-d'œuvre dramatiques de toutes les littératures. Je vous indiquerais les richesses inouïes. J'observe l'histoire des trésors que vous trouvâtes. Je vois la suite! Ma sagesse est aussi dédaignée que le chaos. Qu'est mon néant, auprès de la stupeur qui vous attend?

LIVES

I

O the enormous avenues of the Holy Land, the temple terraces! What has become of the Brahman who explained the proverbs to me? Of that time, of that place, I can still see even the old women! I remember silver hours and sunlight by the rivers, the hand of the country on my shoulder and our caresses standing on the spicy plains.—A flight of scarlet pigeons thunders round my thoughts. An exile here, I once had a stage on which to play all the master-pieces of literature. I would show you unheard-of riches. I note the story of the treasures you discovered. I see the outcome. My wisdom is as scorned as chaos. What is my nothingness to the stupor that awaits you?

II

Je suis un inventeur bien autrement méritant que tous ceux qui m'ont précédé; un musicien même, qui ai trouvé quelque chose comme la clef de l'amour. A présent, gentilhomme d'une campagne aigre au ciel sobre, j'essaye de m'émouvoir au souvenir de l'enfance mendiante, de l'apprentissage ou de l'arrivée en sabots, des polémiques, des cinq ou six veuvages, et de quelques noces où ma forte tête m'empêcha de monter au diapason des camarades. Je ne regrette pas ma vieille part de gaieté divine: l'air sobre de cette aigre campagne alimente fort activement mon atroce scepticisme. Mais comme ce scepticisme ne peut désormais être mis en œuvre, et que d'ailleurs je suis dévoué à un trouble nouveau,—j'attends de devenir un très méchant fou.

III

Dans un grenier où je fus enfermé à douze ans j'ai connu le monde, j'ai illustré la comédie humaine. Dans un cellier j'ai appris l'histoire. A quelque fête de nuit, dans une cité du Nord, j'ai rencontré toutes les femmes des anciens peintres. Dans un vieux passage à

II

I am an inventor more deserving far than all those who have preceded me; a musician, moreover, who has discovered something like the key of love. At present, a country gentleman of a bleak land with a sober sky, I try to rouse myself with the memory of my beggar childhood, my apprenticeship or my arrival in wooden shoes, of polemics, of five or six widowings, and of certain convivialities when my level head kept me from rising to the diapason of my comrades. I do not regret my old portion of divine gaiety: the sober air of this bleak countryside feeds vigorously my dreadful scepticism. But since this scepticism cannot, henceforth, be put to use, and since, moreover, I am dedicated to a new torment,— I expect to become a very vicious madman.

III

In a loft, where I was shut in when I was twelve, I got to know the world, I illustrated the human comedy. I learned history in a wine cellar. In a northern city, at some nocturnal revel, I met all the women of the old masters. In an old arcade in Paris, I was

Paris on m'a enseigné les sciences classiques. Dans une magnifique demeure cernée par l'Orient entier, j'ai accompli mon immense œuvre et passé mon illustre retraite. J'ai brassé mon sang. Mon devoir m'est remis. Il ne faut même plus songer à cela. Je suis réellement d'outre-tombe, et pas de commissions.

taught the classical sciences. In a magnificent dwelling encircled by the entire Orient, I accomplished my prodigious work and spent my illustrious retreat. I churned up my blood. My duty has been remitted. I must not even think of that any more. I am really from beyond the tomb, and no commissions.

DÉPART

Assez vu. La vision s'est rencontrée à tous les airs.

Assez eu. Rumeurs des villes, le soir, et au soleil, et toujours.

Assez connu. Les arrêts de la vie.—O Rumeurs et Visions!

Départ dans l'affection et le bruit neufs.

34

DEPARTURE

Seen enough. The vision was met with in every air.

Had enough. Sounds of cities, in the evening and in the sun and always.

Known enough. Life's halts.—O Sounds and Visions!

Departure in new affection and new noise.

ROYAUTÉ

Un beau matin, chez un peuple fort doux, un homme et une femme superbes criaient sur la place publique: "Mes amis, je veux qu'elle soit reine!" "Je veux être reine!" Elle riait et tremblait. Il parlait aux amis de révélation, d'épreuve terminée. Ils se pâmaient l'un contre l'autre.

En effet, ils furent rois toute une matinée, où les tentures carminées se relevèrent sur les maisons, et toute l'après-midi, où ils s'avancèrent du côté des jardins de palmes.

ROYALTY

One fine morning, in a land of very gentle people, a superb man and woman shouted in the public square: "Friends, I want her to be queen!" "I want to be queen!" She laughed and trembled. He spoke to his friends of revelation, of ordeals terminated. They leaned on each other in ecstasy.

They were indeed sovereigns for a whole morning, while all the houses were adorned with crimson hangings, and for an entire afternoon, while they made their way toward the palm gardens.

A UNE RAISON

Un coup de ton doigt sur le tambour décharge tous les sons et commence la nouvelle harmonie.

Un pas de toi, c'est la levée des nouveaux hommes et leur en-marche.

Ta tête se détourne: le nouvel amour! Ta tête se retourne: le nouvel amour!

"Change nos lots, crible les fléaux, à commencer par le temps", te chantent ces enfants. "Élève n'im-porte où la substance de nos fortunes et de nos vœux", on t'en prie.

Arrivée de toujours, qui t'en iras partout.

TO A REASON

A rap of your finger on the drum fires all the sounds and starts a new harmony.

A step of yours: the levy of new men and their marching on.

Your head turns away: O the new love! Your head turns back: O the new love!

"Change our lots, confound the plagues, beginning with time," to you these children sing. "Raise no matter where the substance of our fortune and our desires," they beg you.

Arrival of all time, who will go everywhere.

MATINÉE D'IVRESSE

O mon Bien! O mon Beau! Fanfare atroce où je ne trébuche point! Chevalet féerique! Hourra pour l'œuvre inouïe et pour le corps merveilleux, pour la première fois! Cela commença sous les rires des enfants, cela finira par eux. Ce poison va rester dans toutes nos veines même quand, la fanfare tournant, nous serons rendu à l'ancienne inharmonie. O maintenant, nous si digne de ces tortures! rassemblons fervemment cette promesse surhumaine faite à notre corps et à notre âme créés: cette promesse, cette démence! L'élégance, la science, la violence! On nous a promis d'enterrer dans l'ombre l'arbre du bien et du mal, de déporter les honnêtetés tyranniques, afin que nous amenions notre très pur amour. Cela commença par quelques dégoûts et cela finit,—ne pouvant nous saisir sur-le-champ de cette éternité,—cela finit par une débandade de parfums.

MORNING OF DRUNKENNESS

O *my* Good! O *my* Beautiful! Appalling fanfare
where I do not falter. Rack of enchantments! Hurrah
for the wonderful work and for the marvelous body,
for the first time! It began in the midst of children's
laughter, with their laughter it will end. This poison
will remain in all our veins even when, the fanfare
turning, we shall be given back to the old dishar-
mony. O now may we, so worthy of these tortures!,
fervently take up that superhuman promise made
to our created body and soul: that promise, that mad-
ness! Elegance, science, violence! They promised to
bury in darkness the tree of good and evil, to deport
tyrannic respectability so that we might bring hither
our very pure love. It began with a certain disgust—
and it ends,—unable instantly to grasp this eternity,
—it ends in a riot of perfumes.

Rire des enfants, discrétion des esclaves, austérité des vierges, horreur des figures et des objets d'ici, sacrés soyez-vous par le souvenir de cette veille. Cela commençait par toute la rustrerie, voici que cela finit par des anges de flamme et de glace.

Petite veille d'ivresse, sainte! quand ce ne serait que pour le masque dont tu nous as gratifié. Nous t'affirmons, méthode! Nous n'oublions pas que tu as glorifié hier chacun de nos âges. Nous avons foi au poison. Nous savons donner notre vie tout entière tous les jours.

Voici le temps des *Assassins*.

Laughter of children, discretion of slaves, austerity of virgins, loathing of faces and objects here, holy be all of you in memory of this vigil. It began with every sort of boorishness, behold it ends with angels of flame and of ice!

Little drunken vigil, holy! if only because of the mask you have bestowed on us. We pronounce you, method! We shall not forget that yesterday you glorified each one of our ages. We have faith in the poison. We know how to give our whole life every day.

Now is the time of the *Assassins.*

PHRASES

Quand le monde sera réduit en un seul bois noir pour nos quatre yeux étonnés,—en une plage pour deux enfants fidèles,—en une maison musicale pour notre claire sympathie,—je vous trouverai.

Qu'il n'y ait ici-bas qu'un vieillard seul, calme et beau, entouré d'un "luxe inouï",—et je suis à vos genoux.

Que j'aie réalisé tous vos souvenirs,—que je sois celle qui sait vous garrotter,—je vous étoufferai.

* * *

Quand nous sommes très forts,—qui recule? très gais,—qui tombe de ridicule? Quand nous sommes très méchants, que ferait-on de nous?

Parez-vous, dansez, riez. Je ne pourrai jamais envoyer l'Amour par la fenêtre.

* * *

PHRASES

When the world is reduced to a single dark wood
for our four eyes' astonishment,—a beach for two
faithful children,—a musical house for our pure sym-
pathy,—I shall find you.

Should there be here below but a single old man,
handsome and calm in the midst of incredible lux-
ury, I shall be at your feet.

Should I have realized all your memories,—should
I be the one who can bind you hand and foot,—I
shall strangle you.

* * *

When we are very strong,—who draws back? very
gay,—who cares for ridicule? When we are very bad,
—what would they do with us?

Deck yourself, dance, laugh. I could never throw
Love out of the window.

* * *

Ma camarade, mendiante, enfant monstre! comme ça t'est égal, ces malheureuses et ces manœuvres, et mes embarras. Attache-toi à nous avec ta voix impossible, ta voix! unique flatteur de ce vil désespoir.

* * *

Une matinée couverte, en juillet. Un goût de cendres vole dans l'air;—une odeur de bois suant dans l'âtre,—les fleurs rouies,—le saccage des promenades,—la bruine des canaux par les champs,—pourquoi pas déjà les joujoux et l'encens?

* * *

J'ai tendu des cordes de clocher à clocher; des guirlandes de fenêtre à fenêtre; des chaînes d'or d'étoile à étoile, et je danse.

* * *

Le haut étang fume continuellement. Quelle sorcière va se dresser sur le couchant blanc? Quelles violettes frondaisons vont descendre?

* * *

Pendant que les fonds publics s'écoulent en fêtes de fraternité, il sonne une cloche de feu rose dans les nuages.

* * *

My comrade, beggar girl, monster child! O it's all one to you these unhappy women, these wiles and my discomfiture. Bind yourself to us with your impossible voice, your voice! sole soother of this vile despair.

* * *

An overcast morning in July. A taste of ashes flies through the air;—an odor of sweating wood on the hearth,—dew-ret flowers—devastation along the promenades—the mist of the canals over the fields— why not incense and toys already?

* * *

I have stretched ropes from steeple to steeple; garlands from window to window; golden chains from star to star, and I dance.

* * *

The upland pond smokes continuously. What witch will rise against the white west sky? What violet frondescence fall?

* * *

While public funds evaporate in feasts of fraternity, a bell of rosy fire rings in the clouds.

* * *

47

Avivant un agréable goût d'encre de Chine, une poudre noire pleut doucement sur ma veillée.—Je baisse les feux du lustre, je me jette sur le lit, et, tourné du côté de l'ombre, je vous vois, mes filles! mes reines!

Reviving a pleasant taste of India ink, a black powder rains on my vigil. I lower the jets of the chandelier, I throw myself on my bed, and turning my face toward the darkness, I see you, my daughters! my queens!

OUVRIERS

O cette chaude matinée de février. Le Sud inop-
portun vint relever nos souvenirs d'indigents absurdes,
notre jeune misère.

Henrika avait une jupe de coton à carreau blanc
et brun, qui a dû être portée au siècle dernier, un bon-
net à rubans et un foulard de soie. C'était bien plus
triste qu'un deuil. Nous faisions un tour dans la ban-
lieue. Le temps était couvert, et ce vent du Sud excitait
toutes les vilaines odeurs des jardins ravagés et des
prés desséchés.

Cela ne devait pas fatiguer ma femme au même
point que moi. Dans une flache laissée par l'inondation
du mois précédent à un sentier assez haut elle me fit
remarquer de très petits poissons.

La ville, avec sa fumée et ses bruits de métiers,
nous suivait très loin dans les chemins. O l'autre
monde, l'habitation bénie par le ciel, et les ombrages!

WORKING PEOPLE

O that warm February morning! The untimely south came to stir up our absurd paupers' memories, our young distress.

Henrika had on a brown and white checked cotton skirt which must have been worn in the last century, a bonnet with ribbons and a silk scarf. It was much sadder than any mourning. We were taking a stroll in the suburbs. The weather was overcast and that wind from the south excited all the evil odors of the desolate gardens and dried fields.

It did not seem to weary my wife as it did me. In a puddle left by the rains of the preceding month, on a fairly high path, she called my attention to some very little fishes.

The city with its smoke and its factory noises followed us far out along the roads. O other world, habitation blessed by sky and shade! The south brought

Le sud me rappelait les misérables incidents de mon enfance, mes désespoirs d'été, l'horrible quantité de force et de science que le sort a toujours éloignée de moi. Non! nous ne passerons pas l'été dans cet avare pays où nous ne serons jamais que des orphelins fiancés. Je veux que ce bras durci ne traîne plus *une chère image*.

back miserable memories of my childhood, my summer despairs, the horrible quantity of strength and of knowledge that fate has always kept from me. No! we will not spend the summer in this avaricious country where we shall never be anything but affianced orphans. I want this hardened arm to stop dragging *a cherished image.*

LES PONTS

Des ciels gris de cristal. Un bizarre dessin de ponts, ceux-ci droits, ceux-là bombés, d'autres descendant ou obliquant en angles sur les premiers; et ces figures se renouvelant dans les autres circuits éclairés du canal, mais tous tellement longs et légers que les rives, chargées de dômes, s'abaissent et s'amoindrissent. Quelques-uns de ces ponts sont encore chargés de masures. D'autres soutiennent des mâts, des signaux, de frêles parapets. Des accords mineurs se croisent, et filent; des cordes montent des berges. On distingue une veste rouge, peut-être d'autres costumes et des instruments de musique. Sont-ce des airs populaires, des bouts de concerts seigneuriaux, des restants d'hymnes publics? L'eau est grise et bleue, large comme un bras de mer.—Un rayon blanc, tombant du haut du ciel, anéantit cette comédie.

THE BRIDGES

Skies the gray of crystal. A strange design of bridges, some straight, some arched, others descending at oblique angles to the first; and these figures recurring in other lighted circuits of the canal, but all so long and light that the banks, laden with domes, sink and shrink. A few of these bridges are still covered with hovels, others support poles, signals, frail parapets. Minor chords cross each other and disappear; ropes rise from the shore. One can make out a red coat, possibly other costumes and musical instruments. Are these popular tunes, snatches of seignioral concerts, remnants of public hymns? The water is gray and blue, wide as an arm of the sea. A white ray falling from high in the sky destroys this comedy.

VILLE

Je suis un éphémère et point trop mécontent citoyen d'une métropole crue moderne, parce que tout goût connu a été éludé dans les ameublements et l'extérieur des maisons aussi bien que dans le plan de la ville. Ici vous ne signaleriez les traces d'aucun monument de superstition. La morale et la langue sont réduites à leur plus simple expression, enfin! Ces millions de gens qui n'ont pas besoin de se connaître amènent si pareillement l'éducation, le métier et la vieillesse, que ce cours de vie doit être plusieurs fois moins long que ce qu'une statistique folle trouve pour les peuples du Continent. Aussi comme, de ma fenêtre, je vois des spectres nouveaux roulant à travers l'épaisse et éternelle fumée de charbon—notre ombre des bois, notre nuit d'été!—des Érinnyes nouvelles, devant mon cottage qui est ma patrie et tout mon cœur puisque tout ici ressemble à ceci,—la Mort sans pleurs, notre active fille et servante, un Amour désespéré et un joli Crime piaulant dans la boue de la rue.

CITY

I am an ephemeral and a not too discontented citizen of a metropolis considered modern because all known taste has been evaded in the furnishings and the exterior of the houses as well as in the layout of the city. Here you would fail to detect the least trace of any monument of superstition. Morals and language are reduced to their simplest expression, at last! The way these millions of people, who do not even need to know each other, manage their education, business, and old age is so identical that the course of their lives must be several times less long than that which a mad statistics calculates for the people of the continent. And from my window I see new specters rolling through the thick eternal smoke —our woodland shade, our summer night!—new Eumenides in front of my cottage which is my country and all my heart since everything here resembles it,—Death without tears, our diligent daughter and servant, a desperate Love, and a pretty Crime howling in the mud of the street.

ORNIÈRES

A droite l'aube d'été éveille les feuilles et les vapeurs et les bruits de ce coin du parc, et les talus de gauche tiennent dans leur ombre violette les mille rapides ornières de la route humide. Défilé de féeries. En effet: des chars chargés d'animaux de bois doré, de mâts et de toiles bariolées, au grand galop de vingt chevaux de cirque tachetés, et les enfants, et les hommes, sur leurs bêtes les plus étonnantes;—vingt véhicules, bossés, pavoisés et fleuris comme des carrosses anciens ou de contes, pleins d'enfants attifés pour une pastorale suburbaine.—Même des cercueils sous leur dais de nuit dressant les panaches d'ébène, filant au trot des grandes juments bleues et noires.

RUTS

To the right the summer dawn wakes the leaves
and the mists and the noises in this corner of the
park, and the left-hand banks hold in their violet
shadows the thousand swift ruts of the wet road.
Wonderland procession! Yes, truly: floats covered
with animals of gilded wood, poles and bright bunt-
ing, to the furious gallop of twenty dappled circus
horses, and children and men on their most fantastic
beasts;—twenty rotund vehicles, decorated with flags
and flowers like the coaches of old or in fairy tales,
full of children all dressed up for a suburban pas-
torale. Even coffins under their somber canopies lift-
ing aloft their jet-black plumes, bowling along to
the trot of huge mares, blue and black.

VILLES

Ce sont des villes! C'est un peuple pour qui se
sont montés ces Alleghanys et ces Libans de rêve!
Des chalets de cristal et de bois qui se meuvent sur
des rails et des poulies invisibles. Les vieux cratères
ceints de colosses et de palmiers de cuivre rugissent
mélodieusement dans les feux. Des fêtes amoureuses
sonnent sur les canaux pendus derrière les chalets. La
chasse des carillons crie dans les gorges. Des corpora-
tions de chanteurs géants accourent dans des vêtements
et des oriflammes éclatants comme la lumière des
cimes. Sur les plates-formes, au milieu des gouffres, les
Rolands sonnent leur bravoure. Sur les passerelles de
l'abîme et les toits des auberges, l'ardeur du ciel
pavoise les mâts. L'écroulement des apothéoses rejoint
les champs des hauteurs où les centauresses séraphiques

CITIES

What cities! This is a people for whom these Alleghenies and these Lebanons of dream were staged! Chalets of crystal and of wood that move along invisible rails and pulleys. Old craters encircled by colossi and copper palms roar melodiously in the fires. Amorous revels ring over the canals pendent behind the chalets. The hunt of chimes clamors in the gorges. Guilds of giant singers congregate in robes and oriflammes as dazzling as the light on mountain peaks. On platforms amidst the precipices Rolands trumpet their valor. On the footbridges over the abyss and on the roofs of inns, the conflagration of the sky decks the masts with flags. The collapse of apotheoses joins the fields and heights where seraphic centauresses wander among the avalanches. Above the level

évoluent parmi les avalanches. Au-dessus du niveau des plus hautes crêtes, une mer troublée par la naissance éternelle de Vénus, chargée de flottes orphéoniques, et de la rumeur des perles et des conques précieuses, la mer s'assombrit parfois avec des éclats mortels. Sur les versants, des moissons de fleurs grandes comme nos armes et nos coupes mugissent. Des cortèges de Mabs en robes rousses, opalines, montent des ravines. Là-haut, les pieds dans la cascade et les ronces, les cerfs tettent Diane. Les Bacchantes des banlieues sanglotent et la lune brûle et hurle. Vénus entre dans les cavernes des forgerons et des ermites. Des groupes de beffrois chantent les idées des peuples. Des châteaux bâtis en os sort la musique inconnue. Toutes les légendes évoluent et les élans se ruent dans les bourgs. Le paradis des orages s'effondre. Les sauvages dansent sans cesse la fête de la nuit. Et, une heure, je suis descendu dans le mouvement d'un boulevard de Bagdad où des compagnies ont chanté la joie du travail nouveau, sous une brise épaisse, circulant sans pouvoir éluder les fabuleux fantômes des monts où l'on a dû se retrouver.

Quels bons bras, quelle belle heure me rendront cette région d'où viennent mes sommeils et mes moindres mouvements?

of the highest peaks, a sea, troubled by the eternal birth of Venus, covered with orpheonic fleets and the murmur of precious conchs and pearls, the sea darkens at times with deadly flashes. On the slopes, harvests of flowers, large as our arms and our goblets, bellow. Processions of Mabs in russet dresses, and opaline, climb the ravines. Up there, with feet in the waterfall and brambles, stags suckle at Diana's breast. Bacchantes of the suburbs sob and the moon burns and bays. Venus enters the caverns of iron-smiths and hermits. Groups of belfries ring out the ideas of the people. Out of castles built of bone comes mysterious music. All the legends advance and elks surge through the towns. The paradise of storms collapses. Savages dance ceaselessly in celebration of the night. And, one hour, I went down into the bustle of a boulevard in Bagdad where companies sang the joy of new toil, in a thick breeze, constantly moving about but unable to elude the fabulous phantoms of the heights, where they were to have met again.

What strong arms, what lovely hour will give me back that region whence come my slumbers and my slightest movements?

VAGABONDS

Pitoyable frère! que d'atroces veillées je lui dus! "Je ne me saisissais pas fervemment de cette entreprise. Je m'étais joué de son infirmité. Par ma faute nous retournerions en exil, en esclavage." Il me supposait un guignon et une innocence très bizarres, et il ajoutait des raisons inquiétantes.

Je répondais en ricanant à ce satanique docteur, et finissais par gagner la fenêtre. Je créais, par delà la campagne traversée par des bandes de musique rare, les fantômes du futur luxe nocturne.

Après cette distraction vaguement hygiénique, je m'étendais sur une paillasse. Et, presque chaque nuit, aussitôt endormi, le pauvre frère se levait, la bouche pourrie, les yeux arrachés—tel qu'il se rêvait! et me tirait dans la salle en hurlant son songe de chagrin idiot.

J'avais en effet, en toute sincérité d'esprit, pris l'en-

VAGABONDS

Pitiful brother! what frightful nights I owed him! "I have not put enough ardor into this enterprise. I have trifled with his infirmity. My fault should we go back to exile, and to slavery." He implied I was unlucky and of a very strange innocence, and would add disquieting reasons.

For reply, I would jeer at this Satanic doctor and, in the end, going over to the window, I would create, beyond the countryside crossed by bands of rare music, phantoms of nocturnal extravagance to come.

After this vaguely hygienic diversion, I would lie down on my pallet and no sooner asleep than, almost every night, the poor brother would rise, his mouth foul, eyes starting from his head,—just as he had dreamed he looked! and would drag me into the room, howling his dream of imbecilic sorrow.

I had, in truth, pledged myself to restore him to

gagement de le rendre à son état primitif de fils du
Soleil,—et nous errions, nourris du vin des cavernes
et du biscuit de la route, moi pressé de trouver le lieu
et la formule.

his primitive state of child of the Sun,—and, nourished by the wine of caverns and the biscuit of the road, we wandered, I impatient to find the place and the formula.

VILLES

L'acropole officielle outre les conceptions de la
barbarie moderne les plus colossales. Impossible
d'exprimer le jour mat produit par ce ciel, immua-
blement gris, l'éclat impérial des bâtisses, et la neige
éternelle du sol. On a reproduit, dans un goût
d'énormité singulier, toutes les merveilles classiques de
l'architecture, et j'assiste à des expositions de peinture
dans des locaux vingt fois plus vastes qu'Hampton-
Court. Quelle peinture! Un Nabuchodonosor norwé-
gien a fait construire les escaliers des ministères; les
subalternes que j'ai pu voir sont déjà plus fiers que des
* * *, et j'ai tremblé à l'aspect des gardiens de co-
losses et officiers de constructions. Par le groupement
des bâtiments en squares, cours et terrasses fermées,
on a evincé les cochers. Les parcs représentent la nature

CITIES

The official acropolis outdoes the most colossal
conceptions of modern barbarity: impossible to de-
scribe the opaque light produced by the immutably
gray sky, the imperial brightness of the buildings,
and the eternal snow on the ground. With a singular
taste for enormity, all the classical marvels of archi-
tecture have been reproduced, and I visit exhibitions
of painting in premises twenty times as vast as
Hampton Court. What painting! A Norwegian
Nebuchadnezzar built the stairways of the govern-
ment buildings; even the subordinates I saw were
already prouder than***, and I trembled at the as-
pect of the guardians of colossi and the building
supervisors. By grouping the buildings around
squares, courts and enclosed terraces, they have
ousted the cabbies. The parks present primitive na-

primitive travaillée par un art superbe, le haut quartier a des parties inexplicables: un bras de mer, sans bateaux, roule sa nappe de grésil bleu entre des quais chargés de candélabres géants. Un pont court conduit à une poterne immédiatement sous le dôme de la Sainte-Chapelle. Ce dôme est une armature d'acier artistique de quinze mille pieds de diamètre environ.

Sur quelques points des passerelles de cuivre, des plates-formes, des escaliers qui contournent les halles et les piliers, j'ai cru pouvoir juger la profondeur de la ville! C'est le prodige dont je n'ai pu me rendre compte: quels sont les niveaux des autres quartiers sur ou sous l'acropole? Pour l'étranger de notre temps, la reconnaissance est impossible. Le quartier commerçant est un circus d'un seul style, avec galeries à arcades. On ne voit pas de boutiques, mais la neige de la chaussée est écrasée; quelques nababs, aussi rares que les promeneurs d'un matin de dimanche à Londres, se dirigent vers une diligence de diamants. Quelques divans de velours rouge: on sert des boissons polaires dont le prix varie de huit cents à huit mille roupies. A l'idée de chercher des théâtres sur ce circus, je me réponds que les boutiques doivent contenir des drames assez sombres. Je pense qu'il y a une police; mais la loi doit être tellement étrange, que je renonce à me faire une idée des aventuriers d'ici.

ture cultivated with superb art, there are parts of the upper town that are inexplicable: an arm of the sea, without boats, rolls its sleet-blue waters between quays covered with giant candelabra. A short bridge leads to a postern directly under the dome of the Sainte-Chapelle. This dome is an artistic structure of steel about fifteen thousand feet in diameter.

From certain points on the copper footbridges, on the platforms, on the stairways that wind around the markets and the pillars, I thought I might form an idea of the depth of the city! This is the prodigy I was unable to discover: what are the levels of the other districts below and above the acropolis? For the stranger of our day exploration is impossible. The business district is a circus in a uniform style with arcaded galleries. No shops are to be seen, but the snow of the roadway is trampled; a few nabobs, as rare as pedestrians on Sunday morning in London, are making their way toward a diamond diligence. A few red velvet divans: polar drinks are served of which the price varies from eight hundred to eight thousand rupees. At the thought of looking for theatres on this circus, I say to myself that the shops must contain dramas quite dismal enough. I suppose there is a police force; but the law must be so strange that I give up trying to imagine what adventurers can be like here.

Le faubourg, aussi élégant qu'une belle rue de Paris, est favorisé d'un air de lumière, l'élément démocratique compte quelque cents âmes. Là encore, les maisons ne se suivent pas; le faubourg se perd bizarrement dans la campagne, le "Comté" qui remplit l'occident éternel des forêts et des plantations prodigieuses où les gentilshommes sauvages chassent leurs chroniques sous la lumière qu'on a créée.

The suburb, as elegant as a beautiful Paris street, is favored with air like light. The democratic element counts a few hundred souls. There, too, the houses do not follow each other; the suburb loses itself queerly in the country, the "County," that fills the eternal west with forests and prodigious plantations where gentlemen savages hunt their news by the light they have invented.

VEILLÉES

I

C'est le repos éclairé, ni fièvre, ni langueur, sur le lit ou sur le pré.

C'est l'ami ni ardent ni faible. L'ami.

C'est l'aimée ni tourmentante ni tourmentée. L'aimée.

L'air et le monde point cherchés. La vie.

—Était-ce donc ceci?

—Et le rêve fraîchit.

74

VIGILS

I

It is repose in the light, neither fever nor languor, on a bed or on a meadow.

It is the friend neither violent nor weak. The friend.

It is the beloved neither tormenting nor tormented. The beloved.

Air and the world not sought. Life.

—Was it really this?

—And the dream grew cold.

II

L'éclairage revient à l'arbre de bâtisse. Des deux extrémités de la salle, décors quelconques, des élévations harmoniques se joignent. La muraille en face du veilleur est une succession psychologique de coupes, de frises, de bandes atmosphériques et d'accidents géologiques.—Rêve intense et rapide de groupes sentimentaux avec des êtres de tous les caractères parmi toutes les apparences.

III

Les lampes et les tapis de la veillée font le bruit des vagues, la nuit, le long de la coque et autour du steerage.

La mer de la veillée, telle que les seins d'Amélie.

Les tapisseries, jusqu'à mi-hauteur, des taillis de dentelle teinte d'émeraude, où se jettent les tourterelles de la veillée.

. . . .

La plaque du foyer noir, de réels soleils des grèves: ah! puits des magies; seule vue d'aurore, cette fois.

76

II

The lighting comes round to the crown post again. From the two extremities of the room—decorations negligible—harmonic elevations join. The wall opposite the watcher is a psychological succession of atmospheric sections of friezes, bands, and geological accidents. Intense quick dream of sentimental groups with people of all possible characters amidst all possible appearances.

III

The lamps and the rugs of the vigil make the noise of waves in the night, along the hull and around the steerage.

The sea of the vigil, like Emily's breasts.

The hangings, halfway up, undergrowth of emerald tinted lace, where dart the vigil doves.

.   .   .   .

The plaque of the black hearth, real suns of seashores; ah! magic wells; only sight of dawn, this time.

77

MYSTIQUE

Sur la pente du talus les anges tournent leurs robes de laine dans les herbages d'acier et d'émeraude.

Des prés de flammes bondissent jusqu'au sommet du mamelon. A gauche le terreau de l'arête est piétiné par tous les homicides et toutes les batailles, et tous les bruits désastreux filent leur courbe. Derrière l'arête de droite, la ligne des orients, des progrès.

Et tandis que la bande en haut du tableau est formée de la rumeur tournante et bondissante des conques des mers et des nuits humaines,

La douceur fleurie des étoiles et du ciel et du reste descend en face du talus, comme un panier,—contre notre face, et fait l'abîme fleurant et bleu là-dessous.

MYSTIC

On the slope of the knoll angels whirl their woolen robes in pastures of emerald and steel.

Meadows of flame leap up to the summit of the little hill. At the left, the mold of the ridge is trampled by all the homicides and all the battles, and all the disastrous noises describe their curve. Behind the right-hand ridge, the line of orients and of progress.

And while the band above the picture is composed of the revolving and rushing hum of seashells and of human nights,

The flowering sweetness of the stars and of the night and all the rest descends, opposite the knoll, like a basket,—against our face, and makes the abyss perfumed and blue below.

AUBE

J'ai embrassé l'aube d'été.

Rien ne bougeait encore au front des palais. L'eau était morte. Les camps d'ombres ne quittaient pas la route du bois. J'ai marché, réveillant les haleines vives et tièdes; et les pierreries regardèrent, et les ailes se levèrent sans bruit.

La première entreprise fut, dans le sentier déjà empli de frais et blêmes éclats, une fleur qui me dit son nom.

Je ris au wasserfall blond qui s'échevela à travers les sapins: à la cime argentée je reconnus la déesse.

Alors je levai un à un les voiles. Dans l'allée, en agitant les bras. Par la plaine, où je l'ai dénoncée au

DAWN

I embraced the summer dawn.

Nothing yet stirred on the face of the palaces. The water was dead. The shadows still camped in the woodland road. I walked, waking quick warm breaths; and gems looked on, and wings rose without a sound.

The first venture was, in a path already filled with fresh, pale gleams, a flower who told me her name.

I laughed at the blond wasserfall that tousled through the pines: on the silver summit I recognized the goddess.

Then, one by one, I lifted up her veils. In the lane, waving my arms. Across the plain, where I

coq. A la grand'ville elle fuyait parmi les clochers et les dômes, et, courant comme un mendiant sur les quais de marbre, je la chassais.

En haut de la route, près d'un bois de lauriers, je l'ai entourée avec ses voiles amassés, et j'ai senti un peu son immense corps. L'aube et l'enfant tombèrent au bas du bois.

Au réveil, il était midi.

notified the cock. In the city, she fled among the steeples and the domes; and running like a beggar on the marble quays, I chased her.

Above the road near a laurel wood, I wrapped her up in her gathered veils, and I felt a little her immense body. Dawn and the child fell down at the edge of the wood.

Waking, it was noon.

FLEURS

D'un gradin d'or,—parmi les cordons de soie, les gazes grises, les velours verts et les disques de cristal qui noircissent comme du bronze au soleil,—je vois la digitale s'ouvrir sur un tapis de filigranes d'argent, d'yeux et de chevelures.

Des pièces d'or jaune semées sur l'agate, des piliers d'acajou supportant un dôme d'émeraudes, des bouquets de satin blanc et de fines verges de rubis entourent la rose d'eau.

Tels qu'un dieu aux énormes yeux bleus et aux formes de neige, la mer et le ciel attirent aux terrasses de marbre la foule des jeunes et fortes roses.

FLOWERS

From a golden step,—among silk cords, green velvets, gray gauzes, and crystal discs that turn black as bronze in the sun, I see the digitalis opening on a carpet of silver filigree, of eyes and hair.

Yellow gold-pieces strewn over agate, mahogany columns supporting emerald domes, bouquets of white satin and delicate sprays of rubies, surround the water-rose.

Like a god with huge blue eyes and limbs of snow, the sea and sky lure to the marble terraces the throng of roses, young and strong.

NOCTURNE VULGAIRE

Un souffle ouvre des brèches opéradiques dans les cloisons,—brouille le pivotement des toits rongés,—disperse les limites des foyers,—éclipse les croisées.

Le long de la vigne, m'étant appuyé du pied à une gargouille,—je suis descendu dans ce carrosse dont l'époque est assez indiquée par les glaces convexes, les panneaux bombés et les sophas contournés. Corbillard de mon sommeil, isolé, maison de berger de ma niaiserie, le véhicule vire sur le gazon de la grande route effacée: et dans un défaut en haut de la glace de droite tournoient les blêmes figures lunaires, feuilles, seins.

—Un vert et un bleu très foncés envahissent l'image.

Dételage aux environs d'une tache de gravier.

—Ici va-t-on siffler pour l'orage, et les Sodomes et les Solymes, et les bêtes féroces et les armées,

COMMON NOCTURNE

A breath opens operatic breaches in the walls,—
blurs the pivoting of crumbling roofs,—disperses
the boundaries of hearths,—eclipses the windows.

Along the vine, having rested my foot on a water-
spout, I climbed down into this coach, its period
indicated clearly enough by the convex panes of
glass, the bulging panels, the contorted sofas. Iso-
lated hearse of my sleep, shepherd's house of my
inanity, the vehicle veers on the grass of the oblit-
erated highway: and in the defect at the top of the
right-hand windowpane revolve pale lunar figures,
leaves, and breasts.

—A very deep green and blue invade the picture.

Unhitching near a spot of gravel.

—Here will they whistle for the storm, and the
Sodoms and Solymas, and the wild beasts and the
armies,

(Postillon et bêtes de songe reprendront-ils sous les plus suffocantés futaies, pour m'enfoncer jusqu'aux yeux dans la source de soie?)

Et nous envoyer, fouettés à travers les eaux clapotantes et les boissons répandues, rouler sur l'aboi des dogues. . .

—Un souffle disperse les limites du foyer.

(Postilion and animals of dream, will they begin
again in the stifling forests to plunge me up to my
eyes in the silken spring?)

And, whipped through the splashing of waters
and spilled drinks, send us rolling on the barking of
bulldogs. . .

—A breath disperses the boundaries of the hearth.

MARINE

Les chars d'argent et de cuivre—
Les proues d'acier et d'argent—
Battent l'écume,—
Soulèvent les souches des ronces.
Les courants de la lande,
Et les ornières immenses du reflux,
Filent circulairement vers l'est,
Vers les piliers de la forêt,—
Vers les fûts de la jetée,
Dont l'angle est heurté par des tourbillons de lumière.

MARINE

Chariots of copper and of silver—
Prows of silver and of steel—
Thresh the foam,—
Upheave the stumps and brambles.
The currents of the heath,
And the enormous ruts of the ebb,
Flow circularly toward the east,
Toward the pillars of the forest,—
Toward the boles of the jetty,
Against whose edge whirlwinds of light collide.

FÊTE D'HIVER

La cascade sonne derrière les huttes d'opéra-comique. Des girandoles prolongent, dans les vergers et les allées voisins du Méandre,—les verts et les rouges du couchant. Nymphes d'Horace coiffées au Premier Empire,—Rondes Sibériennes, Chinoises de Boucher.

WINTER FÊTE

The cascade resounds behind operetta huts. Fireworks prolong, through the orchards and avenues near the Meander,—the greens and reds of the setting sun. Horace nymphs with First Empire headdresses,—Siberian rounds and Boucher's Chinese ladies.

ANGOISSE

Se peut-il qu'Elle me fasse pardonner les ambitions continuellement écrasées,—qu'une fin aisée répare les âges d'indigence,—qu'un jour de succès nous endorme sur la honte de notre inhabileté fatale?

(O palmes! diamant!—Amour, force!—plus haut que toutes joies et gloires!—de toute façon,—partout, démon, dieu,—Jeunesse de cet être-ci: moi!)

Que des accidents de féerie scientifique et des mouvements de fraternité sociale soient chéris comme restitution progressive de la franchise première? . . .

Mais la Vampire qui nous rend gentils commande que nous nous amusions avec ce qu'elle nous laisse, ou qu'autrement nous soyons plus drôles.

Rouler aux blessures, par l'air lassant et la mer; aux supplices, par le silence des eaux et de l'air meurtriers; aux tortures qui rient, dans leur silence atrocement houleux.

94

ANGUISH

Is it possible that She will have me forgiven for ambitions continually crushed,—that an affluent end will make up for the ages of indigence,—that a day of success will lull us to sleep on the shame of our fatal incompetence?

(O palms! diamond!—Love! strength!—higher than all joys and all fame!—in any case, everywhere —demon, god,—Youth of this being: myself!)

That the accidents of scientific wonders and the movements of social brotherhood will be cherished as the progressive restitution of our original freedom? . . .

But the Vampire who makes us behave orders us to enjoy ourselves with what she leaves us, or in other words to be more amusing.

Rolled in our wounds through the wearing air and the sea; in torments through the silence of the murderous waters and air; in tortures that laugh in the terrible surge of their silence.

MÉTROPOLITAIN

Du détroit d'indigo aux mers d'Ossian, sur le sable rose et orange qu'a lavé le ciel vineux, viennent de monter et de se croiser des boulevards de cristal habités incontinent par de jeunes familles pauvres qui s'alimentent chez les fruitiers. Rien de riche.—La ville!

Du désert de bitume fuient droit, en déroute avec les nappes de brumes échelonnées en bandes affreuses au ciel qui se recourbe, se recule et descend formé de la plus sinistre fumée noire que puisse faire l'Océan en deuil, les casques, les roues, les barques, les croupes. —La bataille!

Lève la tête: ce pont de bois, arqué; ces derniers potagers de Samarie; ces masques enluminés sous la lanterne fouettée par la nuit froide; l'ondine niaise à

METROPOLITAN

From the indigo straits to Ossian's seas, on pink and orange sands washed by the vinous sky, crystal boulevards have just risen and crossed, immediately occupied by poor young families who get their food at the greengrocers'. Nothing rich.—The city!

From the bituminous desert, in headlong flight with the sheets of fog spread in frightful bands across the sky, that bends, recedes, descends, formed by the most sinister black smoke that Ocean in mourning can produce, flee helmets, wheels, boats, rumps. —The battle!

Raise your eyes: that arched wooden bridge; those last truck gardens of Samaria; those faces reddened by the lantern lashed by the cold night; silly Undine

la robe bruyante, au bas de la rivière; ces crânes lumineux dans les plans de pois,—et les autres fantasmagories.—La campagne.

Des routes bordées de grilles et de murs, contenant à peine leurs bosquets, et les atroces fleurs qu'on appellerait cœurs et sœurs, Damas damnant de langueur, —possessions de féeriques aristocraties ultra-rhénanes, Japonaises, Guaranies, propres encore à recevoir la musique des anciens,—et il y a des auberges qui, pour toujours, n'ouvrent déjà plus;—il y a des princesses, et, si tu n'es pas trop accablé, l'étude des astres.—Le ciel.

Le matin où, avec Elle, vous vous débattîtes parmi ces éclats de neige, ces lèvres vertes, ces glaces, ces drapeaux noirs et ces rayons bleus, et ces parfums pourpres du soleil des pôles.—Ta force.

in her noisy dress, down by the river; those lumi-
nous skulls among the rows of peas,—and all the
other phantasmagoria—the country.

Roads bordered by walls and iron fences that with
difficulty hold back their groves, and frightful flowers
probably called loves and doves, Damask damning
languorously,—possessions of magic aristocracies
ultra-Rhenish, Japanese, Guaranian, still qualified to
receive ancestral music—and there are inns that now
never open any more,—there are princesses, and if
you are not too overwhelmed, the study of the stars
—the sky.

The morning when with Her you struggled
among the glitterings of snow, those green lips, those
glaciers, black banners and blue beams, and the
purple perfumes of the polar sun.—Your strength.

BARBARE

Bien après les jours et les saisons, et les êtres et les pays,

Le pavillon en viande saignante sur la soie des mers et des fleurs arctiques; (elles n'existent pas).

Remis des vieilles fanfares d'héroïsme,—qui nous attaquent encore le cœur et la tête,—loin des anciens assassins,

—Oh! le pavillon en viande saignante sur la soie des mers et des fleurs arctiques; (elles n'existent pas)—

Douceurs!

Les brasiers, pleuvant aux rafales de givre.—Douceurs!—les feux à la pluie du vent de diamants jetée par le cœur terrestre éternellement carbonisé pour nous.—O monde!

(Loin des vieilles retraites et des vieilles flammes qu'on entend, qu'on sent.)

BARBARIAN

Long after the days and the seasons, and people and countries.

The banner of raw meat against the silk of seas and arctic flowers; (they do not exist).

Recovered from the old fanfares of heroism,—which still attack the heart and head,—far from the old assassins.

—Oh! the banner of raw meat against the silk of seas and arctic flowers; (they do not exist).—

Bliss!

Live embers raining in gusts of frost.—Bliss!—fires in the rain of the wind of diamonds flung out by the earth's heart eternally carbonized for us.—O world!

(Far from the old retreats and the old flames, still heard, still felt.)

Les brasiers et les écumes. La musique, virement des gouffres et chocs des glaçons aux astres.

O douceurs, ô monde, ô musique! Et là, les formes, les sueurs, les chevelures et les yeux, flottant. Et les larmes blanches, bouillantes,—ô douceurs!—et la voix féminine arrivée au fond des volcans et des grottes arctiques.

Le pavillon. . .

Fire and foam. Music, veerings of chasms and clash of icicles against the stars.

O bliss, O world, O music! And forms, sweat, eyes and long hair floating there. And white tears boiling,—O bliss!—and the feminine voice reaching to the bottom of volcanos and grottos of the arctic seas.

The banner. . .

PROMONTOIRE

L'aube d'or et la soirée frissonnante trouvent notre brick en large en face de cette villa et de ses dépendances qui forment un promontoire aussi étendu que l'Épire et le Péloponèse, ou que la grande île du Japon, ou que l'Arabie! Des fanums qu'éclaire la rentrée des théories; d'immenses vues de la défense des côtes modernes; des dunes illustrées de chaudes fleurs et de bacchanales; de grands canaux de Carthage et des Embankments d'une Venise louche; de molles éruptions d'Etnas et des crevasses de fleurs et d'eaux des glaciers; des lavoirs entourés de peupliers d'Allemagne, des talus de parcs singuliers penchant des têtes d'Arbre du Japon; et les façades circulaires des "Royal" ou des "Grand" de Scarbro' et de Brooklyn; et leurs railways flanquent, creusent, surplombent les dispositions de cet Hôtel, choisies dans l'histoire des plus élégantes et des plus colossales constructions de

PROMONTORY

Golden dawn and shivering evening find our brig lying by opposite this villa and its dependencies which form a promontory as extensive as Epirus and the Peloponnesus, or as the large island of Japan, or as Arabia! Fanes lighted up by the return of the *theoriai;* prodigious views of a modern coast's defenses; dunes illustrated with flaming flowers and bacchanalia; grand canals of Carthage and Embankments of a dubious Venice; Etnas languidly erupting, and crevasses of flowers and of glacier waters; washhouses surrounded by German poplars; strange parks with slopes bowing down the heads of the Tree of Japan; and circular façades of the "Grands" and the "Royals" of Scarborough and of Brooklyn; and their railways flank, cut through, and overhang this hotel whose plan was selected in the history of the most elegant and the most colossal edifices of

l'Italie, de l'Amérique et de l'Asie, dont les fenêtres et les terrasses, à présent pleines d'éclairages, de boissons et de brises riches, sont ouvertes à l'esprit des voyageurs et des nobles,—qui permettent, aux heures du jour, à toutes les tarentelles des côtes,—et même aux ritournelles des vallées illustres de l'art de décorer merveilleusement les façades de Palais-Promontoire.

Italy, America, and Asia, and whose windows and terraces, at the moment full of expensive illumination, drinks and breezes, are open to the fancy of the travelers and the nobles who,—during the day allow all the tarantellas of the coast,—and even the ritornels of the illustrious valleys of art, to decorate most wonderfully the façades of Promontory Palace.

SCÈNES

L'ancienne Comédie poursuit ses accords et divise ses Idylles:

Des boulevards de tréteaux.

Un long pier en bois d'un bout à l'autre d'un champ rocailleux où la foule barbare évolue sous les arbres dépouillés.

Dans les corridors de gaze noire, suivant le pas des promeneurs aux lanternes et aux feuilles,

Des oiseaux des mystères s'abattent sur un ponton de maçonnerie mû par l'archipel couvert des embarcations des spectateurs.

Des scènes lyriques, accompagnées de flûte et de

SCENES

Ancient Comedy pursues its harmonies and divides its Idylls:

Raised platforms along the boulevards.

A long wooden pier the length of a rocky field in which the barbarous crowd moves about under the denuded trees.

In corridors of black gauze, following the promenaders with their lanterns and their leaves.

Birds of the mysteries swoop down onto a masonry pontoon, swayed by the sheltered archipelago of spectators' boats.

Operatic scenes with accompaniment of flute and

tambour, s'inclinent dans des réduits ménagés sous les plafonds autour des salons de clubs modernes ou des salles de l'Orient ancien.

La féerie manœuvre au sommet d'un amphithéâtre couronné de taillis,—ou s'agite et module pour les Béotiens, dans l'ombre des futaies mouvantes, sur l'arête des cultures.

L'opéra-comique se divise sur une scène à l'arête d'intersection de dix cloisons dressées de la galerie aux feux.

drum look down from slanting recesses contrived be-
low the ceilings around modern club rooms and halls
of ancient Orient.

The fairy spectacle maneuvers at the top of an
amphitheatre crowned with thickets,—or moves and
modulates for the Boeotians in the shade of waving
forest trees, on the edge of the cultivated fields.

The opéra-comique is divided on a stage at the
line of intersection of ten partitions set up between
the gallery and the footlights.

SOIR HISTORIQUE

En quelque soir, par exemple, que se trouve le touriste naïf, retiré de nos horreurs économiques, la main d'un maître anime le clavecin des prés; on joue aux cartes au fond de l'étang, miroir évocateur des reines et des mignonnes; on a les saintes, les voiles, et les fils d'harmonie, et les chromatismes légendaires, sur le couchant.

Il frissonne au passage des chasses et des hordes. La comédie goutte sur les tréteaux de gazon. Et l'embarras des pauvres et des faibles sur ces plans stupides!

A sa vision esclave, l'Allemagne s'échafaude vers des lunes; les déserts tartares s'éclairent; les révoltes anciennes grouillent dans le centre du Céleste Empire; par les escaliers et les fauteuils de rocs, un petit monde blême et plat, Afrique et Occidents, va s'édifier. Puis un ballet de mers et de nuits connues, une chimie sans valeur, et des mélodies impossibles.

HISTORIC EVENING

On an evening, for example, when the naïve tourist has retired from our economic horrors, a master's hand awakes the meadow's harpsichord; they are playing cards at the bottom of the pond, mirror conjuring up favorites and queens; there are saints, veils, threads of harmony, and legendary chromatisms in the setting sun.

He shudders as the hunts and hordes go by. Comedy drips on the grass stages. And the distress of the poor and of the weak on those stupid planes!

Before his slave's vision, Germany goes scaffolding toward moons; Tartar deserts light up; ancient revolts ferment in the center of the Celestial Empire; over stairways and armchairs of rock, a little world, wan and flat, Africa and Occidents, will be erected. Then a ballet of familiar seas and nights, worthless chemistry and impossible melodies.

La même magie bourgeoise à tous les points où la malle nous déposera! Le plus élémentaire physicien sent qu'il n'est plus possible de se soumettre à cette atmosphère personnelle, brume de remords physiques, dont la constatation est déjà une affliction.

Non! Le moment de l'étuve, des mers enlevées, des embrasements souterrains, de la planète emportée, et des exterminations conséquentes, certitudes si peu malignement indiquées dans la Bible et par les Nornes et qu'il sera donné à l'être sérieux de surveiller.—Cependant ce ne sera point un effet de légende!

The same bourgeois magic wherever the mail-train sets you down. Even the most elementary physicist feels that it is no longer possible to submit to this personal atmosphere, fog of physical remorse, which to acknowledge is already an affliction.

No! The moment of the seething caldron, of seas removed, of subterranean conflagrations, of the planet swept away, and the consequent exterminations, certitudes indicated with so little malice by the Bible and by the Nornes and for which serious persons should be on the alert. Yet there will be nothing legendary about it.

MOUVEMENT

Le mouvement de lacet sur la berge des chutes du
    fleuve,
Le gouffre à l'étambot,
La célérité de la rampe,
L'énorme passade du courant
Mènent par les lumières inouïes
Et la nouveauté chimique
Les voyageurs entourés des trombes du val
Et du strom.

Ce sont les conquérants du monde
Cherchant la fortune chimique personnelle;
Le sport et le confort voyagent avec eux;
Ils emmènent l'éducation
Des races, des classes et des bêtes, sur ce vaisseau
Repos et vertige
A la lumière diluvienne
Aux terribles soirs d'étude.

MOTION

The swaying motion on the banks of the river falls
The vortex at the sternpost,
The swiftness of the rail,
The vast passage of the current
Conduct through unimaginable lights
And chemical change
The travelers surrounded by waterspouts of the strath
And of the strom.

They are the conquerors of the world.
Seeking their personal chemical fortune;
Sports and comforts voyage with them;
They carry the education
Of races, classes and of animals, on this ship
Repose and dizziness
To torrential light
To terrible nights of study.

Car de la causerie parmi les appareils, le sang, les
    fleurs, le feu, les bijoux,
Des comptes agités à ce bord fuyard,
—On voit, roulant comme une digue au-delà de la
    route hydraulique motrice,
Monstrueux, s'éclairant sans fin,—leur stock
    d'études;
Eux chassés dans l'extase harmonique,
Et l'héroïsme de la découverte.

Aux accidents atmosphériques les plus surprenants,
Un couple de jeunesse s'isole sur l'arche,
—Est-ce ancienne sauvagerie qu'on pardonne?—
Et chante et se poste.

For from the talk among the apparatus, the blood,
    the flowers, the fire, the gems,
From the excited calculations on this fugitive ship,
—One sees, rolling like a dyke beyond the hydraulic-
    power road,
Monstrous, endlessly illuminated,—their stock of
    studies;
They driven into harmonic ecstasy,
And the heroism of discovery.

In the most startling atmospheric accidents,
A youthful couple holds itself aloof on the ark,
—Is it primitive shyness that people pardon?—
And sings and stands guard.

BOTTOM

La réalité étant trop épineuse pour mon grand caractère,—je me trouvai néanmoins chez ma dame, en gros oiseau gris-bleu s'essorant vers les moulures du plafond et traînant l'aile dans les ombres de la soirée.

Je fus, au pied du baldaquin supportant ses bijoux adorés et ses chefs-d'œuvre physiques, un gros ours aux gencives violettes et au poil chenu de chagrin, les yeux aux cristaux et aux argents des consoles.

Tout se fit ombre et aquarium ardent.

Au matin,—aube de juin batailleuse,—je courus aux champs, âne, claironnant et brandissant mon grief, jusqu'à ce que les Sabines de la banlieue vinrent se jeter à mon poitrail.

BOTTOM

Reality being too thorny for my great personality.
—I found myself nevertheless at my lady's, an enormous gray-blue bird soaring toward the moldings of the ceiling and trailing my wings through the shadows of the evening.

At the foot of the canopy supporting her adored gems and her physical masterpieces, I was a great bear with violet gums, fur hoary with sorrow, eyes on the silver and crystal of the consoles.

Everything became shadow and ardent aquarium.

In the morning,—bellicose dawn of June,—a donkey, I rushed into the fields, braying and brandishing my grievance, until the Sabine women of the suburbs came and threw themselves on my neck.

H

Toutes les monstruosités violent les gestes atroces
d'Hortense. Sa solitude est la mécanique érotique; sa
lassitude, la dynamique amoureuse. Sous la surveillance
d'une enfance, elle a été, à des époques nombreuses,
l'ardente hygiène des races. Sa porte est ouverte à la
misère. Là, la moralité des êtres actuels se décorpore
en sa passion ou en son action.—O terrible frisson des
amours novices sur le sol sanglant et par l'hydrogène
clarteux!—trouvez Hortense.

H

Every monstrosity violates the atrocious gestures
of Hortense. Erotic mechanics, her solitude; her
lassitude, amorous dynamics. Under childhood's
guidance she has been, in numerous ages, the ar-
dent hygiene of all races. Her door is open to mis-
ery. There, the morality of living beings is disem-
bodied in her passion or her action.—O terrible shud-
der of novice loves on the bloody ground and in the
transparent hydrogen!—find Hortense.

DÉVOTION

A ma sœur Louise Vanaen de Voringhem:—Sa cornette bleue tournée à la mer du Nord.—Pour les naufragés.

A ma sœur Léonie Aubois d'Ashby. Baou—l'herbe d'été bourdonnante et puante.—Pour la fièvre des mères et des enfants.

A Lulu,—démon—qui a conservé un goût pour les oratoires du temps des Amies et de son éducation incomplète. Pour les hommes!—A madame * * *.

A l'adolescent que je fus. A ce saint vieillard, ermitage ou mission.

DEVOTIONS

To Sister Louise Vanaen de Voringhem:—Her blue coif turned toward the North Sea.—For the shipwrecked.

To Sister Léonie Aubois d'Ashby. Baou—the buzzing, stinking summer grass.—For the fever of mothers and children.

To Lulu,—demon—who has kept a taste for the oratories of the time of *Les Amies* and her unfinished education. For men!—To Madame* * *.

To the adolescent I was. To that holy old man, hermitage or mission.

'A l'esprit des pauvres. Et à un très haut clergé.

Aussi bien, à tout culte en telle place de culte mémoriale et parmi tels événements qu'il faille se rendre, suivant les aspirations du moment ou bien notre propre vice sérieux.

Ce soir, à Circeto des hautes glaces, grasse comme le poisson, et enluminée comme les dix mois de la nuit rouge—(son cœur ambre et spunk),—pour ma seule prière muette comme ces régions de nuit, et précédant des bravoures plus violentes que ce chaos polaire.

A tout prix et avec tous les airs, même dans des voyages métaphysiques.—Mais plus *alors*.

To the spirit of the poor. And to a very high clergy.

As well as to all cults in any place of memorial cults and amidst any events to which one must succumb according to the aspirations of the moment or one's own serious vice.

This evening to Circeto of the icy heights, fat as a fish, and painted like the ten months of the red night—(her heart amber and spunk),—for my only prayer silent as those nocturnal regions, and preceding feats more violent than this chaos of the poles.

No matter how, no matter where, even in metaphysical journeys.—But *then* no more.

DÉMOCRATIE

"Le drapeau va au paysage immonde, et notre patois étouffe le tambour.

"Aux centres nous alimenterons la plus cynique prostitution. Nous massacrerons les révoltes logiques.

"Aux pays poivrés et détrempés!—au service des plus monstrueuses exploitations industrielles ou militaires.

"Au revoir ici, n'importe où. Conscrits du bon vouloir, nous aurons la philosophie féroce; ignorants pour la science, roués pour le confort; la crevaison pour le monde qui va. C'est la vraie marche. En avant, route!"

DEMOCRACY

"The flag goes with the foul landscape, and our jargon muffles the drum.

"In the great centers we'll nurture the most cynical prostitution. We'll massacre logical revolts.

"In spicy and drenched lands!—at the service of the most monstrous exploitations, industrial or military.

"Farewell here, no matter where. Conscripts of good will, ours will be a ferocious philosophy; ignorant as to science, rabid for comfort; and let the rest of the world croak. This is the real advance. Marching orders, let's go!"

.

FAIRY

Pour Hélène se conjurèrent les sèves ornementales dans les ombres vierges et les clartés impassibles dans le silence astral. L'ardeur de l'été fut confiée à des oiseaux muets et l'indolence requise à une barque de deuils sans prix par des anses d'amours morts et de parfums affaissés.

—Après le moment de l'air des bûcheronnes à la rumeur du torrent sous la ruine des bois, de la sonnerie des bestiaux à l'écho des vals, et des cris des steppes.—

Pour l'enfance d'Hélène frissonnèrent les fourrures et les ombres, et le sein des pauvres, et les légendes du ciel,

Et ses yeux et sa danse supérieurs encore aux éclats précieux, aux influences froides, au plaisir du décor et de l'heure uniques.

FAIRY

For Helen, in the virgin shadows and the impassive radiance in astral silence, ornamental saps conspired. Summer's ardor was confided to silent birds and due indolence to a priceless mourning boat through gulfs of dead loves and fallen perfumes.

—After the moment of the woodswomen's song to the rumble of the torrent in the ruin of the wood, of the tinkle of the cowbells to the echo of the vales, and the cries of the steppes.—

For Helen's childhood, furs and shadows trembled, and the breast of the poor and the legends of heaven.

And her eyes and her dance superior even to the precious radiance, to cold influences, to the pleasure of the unique setting and the unique hour.

GUERRE

Enfant, certains ciels ont affiné mon optique: tous
les caractères nuancèrent ma physionomie. Les Phé-
nomènes s'émurent.—A présent, l'inflexion éternelle
des moments et l'infini des mathématiques me chas-
sent par ce monde où je subis tous les succès civils,
respecté de l'enfance étrange et des affections énormes.
—Je songe à une Guerre, de droit ou de force, de
logique bien imprévue.

C'est aussi simple qu'une phrase musicale.

WAR

When a child, certain skies sharpened my vision: all their characters were reflected in my face. The Phenomena were roused.—At present, the eternal inflection of moments and the infinity of mathematics drives me through this world where I meet with every civil honor, respected by strange children and prodigious affections.—I dream of a War of right and of might, of unlooked-for logic.

It is as simple as a musical phrase.

GENIE

Il est l'affection et le présent puisqu'il a fait la maison ouverte à l'hiver écumeux et à la rumeur de l'été—lui qui a purifié les boissons et les aliments—lui qui est le charme des lieux fuyants et le délice surhumain des stations.—Il est l'affection et l'avenir, la force et l'amour que nous, debout dans les rages et les ennuis, nous voyons passer dans le ciel de tempête et les drapeaux d'extase.

Il est l'amour, mesure parfaite et réinventée, raison merveilleuse et imprévue, et l'éternité: machine aimée des qualités fatales. Nous avons tous eu l'épouvante de sa concession et de la nôtre: ô jouissance de notre santé, élan de nos facultés, affection égoïste et passion pour lui,—lui qui nous aime pour sa vie infinie. . .

Et nous nous le rappelons et il voyage. . . Et si l'Adoration s'en va, sonne, sa promesse sonne: "Ar-

GENIE

He is affection and the present since he has made the house open to foamy winter and to the murmur of summer—he who has purified food and drink— he who is the charm of fleeing places and the super- human delight of stations.—He is affection and the future, love and strength whom we, standing in our rages and our boredoms, see passing in the stormy sky and banners of ecstasy.

He is love, perfect measure reinvented, marvelous and unlooked-for reason, and eternity: loved instru- ment of fatal qualities. We all have known the terror of his concession and of ours: O relish of health, the soaring of our faculties, selfish affection and passion for him,—for him who loves us for his infinite life. . .

And we remember him and he has gone on a journey. . . And if Adoration goes, rings, his prom- ise rings: "Away these superstitions, these ancient

rière ces superstitions, ces anciens corps, ces ménages et ces âges. C'est cette époque-ci qui a sombré!"

Il ne s'en ira pas, il ne redescendra pas d'un ciel, il n'accomplira pas la rédemption des colères de femmes et des gaietés des hommes et de tout ce péché: car c'est fait, lui étant, et étant aimé.

O ses souffles, ses têtes, ses courses: la terrible célérité de la perfection des formes et de l'action.

O fécondité de l'esprit et immensité de l'univers!

Son corps! le dégagement rêvé, le brisement de la grâce croisée de violence nouvelle! sa vue, sa vue! tous les agenouillages anciens et les peines *relevés* à sa suite.

Son jour! l'abolition de toutes souffrances sonores et mouvantes dans la musique plus intense.

Son pas! les migrations plus énormes que les anciennes invasions.

O lui et nous! l'orgueil plus bienveillant que les charités perdues.

O monde! et le chant clair des malheurs nouveaux!

Il nous a connus tous et nous a tous aimés: sachons, cette nuit d'hiver, de cap en cap, du pôle tumultueux

bodies, these couples, and these ages. It is this epoch that has foundered!"

He will not go away, he will not come down again from any heaven, he will not accomplish the redemption of the angers of women and the gaieties of men or of all this sin: for it is done, he being, and being loved.

O his breaths, his heads, his flights: terrible celerity of the perfection of forms and of action.

O fecundity of the mind and immensity of the universe!

His body! the dreamed-of release, the shattering of grace crossed by new violence! His vision, his vision! all the old kneelings and the pains *raised* at his passing.

His day! the abolition of all resounding and restless sufferings in intenser music.

His step! migrations more vast than the ancient invasions.

O he and we! Pride more compassionate than the lost charities.

O world and the pure song of new evils!

He has known us all and all of us has loved: Take heed this winter night, from cape to cape, from the

au château, de la foule à la plage, de regards en regards, forces et sentiments las, le héler et le voir, et le renvoyer, et, sous les marées et au haut des déserts de neige, suivre ses vues,—ses souffles,—son corps,—son jour.

tumultuous pole to the castle, from the crowd to the shore, from glance to glance, force and feelings weary, to hail him, to see him and to send him away, and under the tides and high in the deserts of snow, to follow his visions,—his breaths,—his body,—his day.

JEUNESSE

I

Dimanche

Les calculs de côté, l'inévitable descente du ciel et
la visite des souvenirs et la séance des rhythmes occu-
pent la demeure, la tête et le monde de l'esprit.

—Un cheval détale sur le turf suburbain, et le long
des cultures et des boisements, percé par la peste car-
bonique. Une misérable femme de drame, quelque
part dans le monde, soupire après des abandons im-
probables. Les desperadoes languissent après l'orage,
l'ivresse et les blessures. De petits enfants étouffent des
malédictions le long des rivières.

Reprenons l'étude au bruit de l'œuvre dévorante
qui se rassemble et remonte dans les masses.

YOUTH

I

Sunday

Problems put by, the inevitable descent of heaven and the visit of memories and the assembly of rhythms occupy the house, the head and the world of the spirit.

—A horse scampers off on the suburban track, and along the tilled fields and woodlands, pervaded by the carbonic plague. A miserable woman of drama, somewhere in the world, sighs for improbable desertions. Desperados pine for strife, drunkenness and wounds.—Little children stifle their maledictions along the rivers.

Let us resume our study to the noise of the consuming work that is gathering and growing in the masses.

II

Sonnet

Homme de constitution ordinaire, la chair n'était-elle pas un fruit pendu dans le verger, ô journées enfantes! le corps un trésor à prodiguer; ô aimer, le péril ou la force de Psyché? La terre avait des versants fertiles en princes et en artistes, et la descendance et la race vous poussaient aux crimes et aux deuils: le monde, votre fortune et votre péril. Mais à présent, ce labeur comblé, toi, tes calculs,—toi, tes impatiences —ne sont plus que votre danse et votre voix, non fixées et point forcées, quoique d'un double événement d'invention et de succès une raison,—en l'humanité fraternelle et discrète par l'univers sans images; —la force et le droit réfléchissent la danse et la voix à présent seulement appréciées.

III

Vingt Ans

Les voix instructives exilées. . . L'ingénuité physique amèrement rassise. . . —Adagio.—Ah! l'é-

II

Sonnet

Man of ordinary constitution, was not the flesh a fruit hanging in the orchard; O child days; the body, a treasure to squander; O to love, the peril or the power of Psyche? The earth had slopes fertile in princes and in artists, and lineage and race incited you to crimes and mournings: the world, your fortune and your peril. But now, that labor crowned, you and your calculations,—you and your impatiences—are only your dance and your voice, not fixed and not forced, although a reason for the double consequence of invention and of success,— in fraternal and discreet humanity . through an imageless universe;—might and right reflect your dance and your voice, appreciated only at present.

III

Twenty Years Old

Instructive voices exiled. . . Physical candor bitterly quelled. . . —Adagio.—Ah! the infinite ego-

143

goïsme infini de l'adolescence, l'optimisme studieux:
que le monde était plein de fleurs cet été! Les airs et
les formes mourant. . . —Un chœur, pour calmer
l'impuissance et l'absence! Un chœur de verres, de
mélodies nocturnes. . . En effet, les nerfs vont vite
chasser.

IV

Tu en es encore à la tentation d'Antoine. L'ébat du
zèle écourté, les tics d'orgueil puéril, l'affaissement et
l'effroi.

Mais tu te mettras à ce travail: toutes les possibili-
tés harmoniques et architecturales s'émouvront autour
de ton siège. Des êtres parfaits, imprévus, s'offriront
à tes expériences. Dans tes environs affluera rêveuse-
ment la curiosité d'anciennes foules et de luxes oisifs.
Ta mémoire et tes sens ne seront que la nourriture de
ton impulsion créatrice. Quant au monde, quand tu
sortiras, que sera-t-il devenu? En tout cas, rien des
apparences actuelles.

tism of adolescence, the studious optimism: how the world was full of flowers that summer! Airs and forms dying. . . —A choir to calm impotence and absence! A choir of glasses, of nocturnal melodies. . . Quickly, indeed, the nerves take up the chase.

IV

You are still at Anthony's temptation. The antics of abated zeal, the grimaces of childish pride, the collapse and the terror.

But you will set yourself this labor: all harmonic and architectural possibilities will surge around your seat. Perfect beings, never dreamed of, will present themselves for your experiments. The curiosity of ancient crowds and idle wealth will meditatively draw near. Your memory and your senses will be simply the nourishment of your creative impulse. As for the world, when you emerge, what will it have become? In any case, nothing of what it seems at present.

SOLDE

A vendre ce que les Juifs n'ont pas vendu, ce que noblesse ni crime n'ont goûté, ce qu'ignorent l'amour maudit et la probité infernale des masses! ce que le temps ni la science n'ont pas à reconnaître:

Les Voix reconstituées; l'éveil fraternel de toutes les énergies chorales et orchestrales et leurs applications instantanées; l'occasion, unique, de dégager nos sens!

A vendre les Corps sans prix, hors de toute race, de tout monde, de tout sexe, de toute descendance! Les richesses jaillissant à chaque démarche! Solde de diamants sans contrôle!

A vendre l'anarchie pour les masses; la satisfaction irrépressible pour les amateurs supérieurs; la mort atroce pour les fidèles et les amants!

SALE

For sale what the Jews have not sold, what neither nobility nor crime have tasted, what is unknown to monstrous love and to the infernal probity of the masses! what neither time nor science need recognize:

The Voices restored; fraternal awakening of all choral and orchestral energies and their instantaneous application; the opportunity, the only one, for the release of our senses!

For sale Bodies without price, outside any race, any world, any sex, any lineage! Riches gushing at every step! Uncontrolled sale of diamonds!

For sale anarchy for the masses; irrepressible satisfaction for rare connoisseurs; agonizing death for the faithful and for lovers!

A vendre les habitations et les migrations, sports, féeries et conforts parfaits, et le bruit, le mouvement et l'avenir qu'ils font!

A vendre les applications de calcul et les sauts d'harmonie inouïs. Les trouvailles et les termes non soupçonnés,—possession immédiate.

Élan insensé et infini aux splendeurs invisibles, aux délices insensibles,—et ses secrets affolants pour chaque vice—et sa gaieté effrayante pour la foule.

A vendre les corps, les voix, l'immense opulence inquestionable, ce qu'on ne vendra jamais. Les vendeurs ne sont pas à bout de solde! Les voyageurs n'ont pas à rendre leur commission de si tôt.

For sale colonizations and migrations, sports, fairylands and incomparable comforts, and the noise and the movement and the future they make!

For sale the application of calculations and the incredible leaps of harmony. Discoveries and terms never dreamed of,—immediate possession.

Wild and infinite flight toward invisible splendors, toward intangible delights—and its maddening secrets for every vice—and its terrifying gaiety for the mob.

For sale, the bodies, the voices, the enormous and unquestionable wealth, that which will never be sold. Salesmen are not at the end of their stock! It will be some time before travelers have to turn in their accounts.

OTHER PROSE POEMS

LES DÉSERTS DE L'AMOUR

AVERTISSEMENT

Ces écritures-ci sont d'un jeune, tout jeune homme, *dont la vie s'est développée n'importe où; sans mère, sans pays, insoucieux de tout ce qu'on connaît, fuyant toute force morale, comme furent déjà plusieurs pitoyables jeunes hommes. Mais, lui, si ennuyé et si troublé, qu'il ne fit que s'amener à la mort comme à une pudeur terrible et fatale. N'ayant pas aimé de femmes,—quoique plein de sang!—il eut son âme et son cœur, toute sa force, élevés en des erreurs étranges et tristes. Des rêves suivants,—ses amours! —qui lui vinrent dans ses lits ou dans les rues, et de leur suite et de leur fin, de douces considérations religieuses se dégagent peut-être. Se rappellera-t-on le sommeil continu des Mahométans légendaires,— braves pourtant et circoncis! Mais, cette bizarre souf- france possédant une autorité inquiétante, il faut sin-*

THE DESERTS OF LOVE

FOREWORD

These are the writings of a young, a very young man, who has grown up anywhere; without mother, without country, indifferent to everything other people know, fleeing all moral courage, like many other pitiful young men before him. But he, so full of anxiety and so troubled, did nothing but set his course toward death as toward a terrible and fatal decency. Not having loved women,—fullblooded though he was!—his soul and his heart, all his strength, were taken up with aberrations, strange and sad. The following dreams,—his loves!—that came to him in his beds and in the streets, and from their sequence and from their ending sweet religious considerations may arise. Who will recall the continuous sleep of the legendary Mohammedans,—brave though and circumcised! But this fantastic suffering

cèrement désirer que cette Ame, égarée parmi nous tous, et qui veut la mort, ce semble, rencontre en cet instant-là des consolations sérieuses et soit digne.

I

Cette fois, c'est la Femme que j'ai vue dans la Ville, et à qui j'ai parlé et qui me parle.

J'étais dans une chambre, sans lumière. On vint me dire qu'elle était chez moi: et je la vis dans mon lit, toute à moi, sans lumière! Je fus très-ému, et beaucoup parce que c'était la maison de famille: aussi une détresse me prit! J'étais en haillons, moi, et elle, mondaine qui se donnait: il lui fallait s'en aller! Une détresse sans nom: je la pris, et la laissai tomber hors du lit, presque nue; et, dans ma faiblesse indicible, je tombai sur elle et me traînai avec elle parmi les tapis, sans lumière! La lampe de la famille rougissait l'une après l'autre les chambres voisines. Alors, la femme disparut. Je versai plus de larmes que Dieu n'en a jamais pu demander.

Je sortis dans la ville sans fin. O fatigue! Noyé dans la nuit sourde et dans la fuite du bonheur.

possessing a disturbing sovereignty, it is sincerely to be hoped that this Soul, among us lost, and who desires death, it seems, should meet at that instant authentic consolations and be worthy.

I

This time it is the Woman whom I saw in the City, and to whom I have spoken and who speaks to me.

I was in a room without light. They came to tell me she was there; and I saw her in my bed, all mine, without light! I was troubled, and largely because it was my parents' house, so anguish filled me! I was in rags while she, a woman of the world, was giving herself to me: she would have to go away! A nameless anguish: I took her, and let her fall from the bed, almost naked; and, in my unutterable weakness, I fell upon her and rolled with her on the rugs, without light! The family lamp reddened one by one the adjoining rooms. Then, the woman disappeared. I shed more tears than God could ever have required.

I went out into the city without end. O weariness! Drowned in the insensible night and in the flight of

C'était comme une nuit d'hiver, avec une neige pour
étouffer le monde décidément. Les amis, auxquels je
criais: où reste-t-elle? répondaient faussement. Je fus
devant les vitrages de là où elle va tous les soirs: je
courais dans un jardin enseveli. On m'a repoussé. Je
pleurais énormément, à tout cela. Enfin, je suis des-
cendu dans un lieu plein de poussière, et, assis sur
des charpentes, j'ai laissé finir toutes les larmes de
mon corps avec cette nuit.—Et mon épuisement me
revenait pourtant toujours.

J'ai compris qu'Elle était à sa vie de tous les jours;
et que le tour de bonté serait plus long à se reproduire
qu'une étoile. Elle n'est pas revenue, et ne reviendra
jamais, l'Adorable qui s'était rendue chez moi,—ce
que je n'aurais jamais présumé. Vrai, cette fois j'ai
pleuré plus que tous les enfants du monde.

II

C'est, certes, la même campagne. La même
maison rustique de mes parents: la salle même où les
dessus de portes sont des bergeries roussies, avec des
armes et des lions. Au dîner, il y a un salon avec des
bougies et des vins et des boiseries antiques. La table

happiness. It was like a winter night with a fall of snow to smother the world once and for all. The friends to whom I cried: Where is she? falsely replied. I was there in front of the windows where she goes every evening. I was running through a buried garden. They drove me away. At all this I wept prodigiously. Finally, I went down into a place filled with dust and, sitting on some lumber, I drained my body of all its tears that night.—And yet always my exhaustion returned.

I understood that She belonged to her everyday life; and that it would take longer for the turn of kindness to come again than for the reproduction of a star. She has not returned and will never return, the Adorable One, who visited me in my home,—something I should never have presumed to ask. True, this time, I wept more than all the children in the world.

II

It is certainly the same countryside. The same rustic house of my parents: even the same room where the overdoors are russet sheepfolds with lions and coats of arms. At dinner, there is a room with candles and wines and antique paneling. The dining

à manger est très-grande. Les servantes! elles étaient plusieurs, autant que je m'en suis souvenu.—Il y avait là un de mes jeunes amis anciens, prêtre et vêtu en prêtre; maintenant: c'était pour être plus libre. Je me souviens de sa chambre de pourpre, à vitres de papier jaune: et ses livres, cachés, qui avaient trempé dans l'océan!

Moi, j'étais abandonné, dans cette maison de campagne sans fin: lisant dans la cuisine, séchant la boue de mes habits devant les hôtes, aux conversations du salon: ému jusqu'à la mort par le murmure du lait du matin et de la nuit du siècle dernier.

J'étais dans une chambre très sombre: que faisais-je? Une servante vint près de moi: je puis dire que c'était un petit chien: quoiqu'elle fût belle, et d'une noblesse maternelle inexprimable pour moi: pure, connue, toute charmante! Elle me pinça le bras.

Je ne me rappelle même plus bien sa figure: ce n'est pas pour me rappeler son bras, dont je roulai la peau dans mes deux doigts; ni sa bouche, que la mienne saisit comme une petite vague désespérée, minant sans fin quelque chose. Je la renversai dans une corbeille de coussins et de toiles de navire, en un

158

table is very large. The servants! there were several as far as I can remember.—One of my young friends of old was there, a priest and dressed like a priest; at present: for the sake of greater freedom. I remember his purple room with yellow paper panes; and his hidden books that had soaked in the sea!

As for me, I was abandoned in that country house without end; reading in the kitchen, drying the mud of my clothes in front of the guests with their drawing-room conversation: mortally troubled by the murmur of the milk of morning and the night of the last century.

I was in a very dark room: what was I doing? A little servant girl came toward me: a puppy I should say: notwithstanding she was beautiful, noble and maternal beyond words to me: pure, familiar, altogether charming. She pinched my arm.

I can no longer remember even her face very well: much less her arm whose flesh I rolled between my fingers; nor her mouth which mine seized like a desperate little wave endlessly lapping. I flung her onto a basket of cushions and sail cloth in a dark

coin noir. Je ne me rappelle plus que son pantalon à dentelles blanches.

Puis, ô désespoir! la cloison devint vaguement l'ombre des arbres, et je me suis abîmé sous la tristesse amoureuse de la nuit.

corner. And I remember nothing but her white drawers trimmed with lace.

Then, O despair! The wall became dimly the shadow of trees, and I was plunged in the amorous sadness of the night.

TROIS MÉDITATIONS JOHANNIQUES

À SAMARIE

A Samarie, plusieurs ont manifesté leur foi en lui. Il ne les a pas vus. Samarie la parvenue, l'égoïste, plus rigide observatrice de sa loi protestante que Juda des tables antiques. Là la richesse universelle permettait toute discussion éclairée. Le sophisme, esclave et soldat de la routine, y avait déjà, après les avait flattés, égorgé plusieurs prophètes.

C'était un mot sinistre, celui de la femme à la fontaine: "Vous êtes prophètes, vous savez ce que j'ai fait."

Les femmes et les hommes croyaient aux prophètes. Maintenant on croit à l'homme d'état.

A deux pas de la ville étrangère, incapable de la menacer matériellement, s'il était pris comme prophète, puisqu'il s'était montré là si bizarre, qu'aurait-il fait?

Jésus n'a rien pu dire à Samarie.

THREE GOSPEL MORALITIES

IN SAMARIA

In Samaria quite a few people manifested their faith in him. He did not see them. Samaria, the upstart, the egoist, a stricter observer of protestant law than Judea of its ancient tables. There the universal wealth sanctioned all enlightened discussion. Sophism, routine's slave and soldier, had already, after flattering several prophets, cut their throats.

They were ominous words, those of the woman at the well: "You are a prophet, you know what I have done."

The women and the men believed in prophets. Today people believe in statesmen.

Not a stone's throw from the strange city and unable to threaten it physically, suppose he had been taken for a prophet, since he had behaved so queerly there, what would he have done?

Jesus was not able to say anything in Samaria.

163

EN GALILÉE

L'air léger et charmant de la Galilée: les habitants
le reçurent avec une joie curieuse: ils l'avaient vu,
secoué par la sainte colère, fouetter les changeurs et
les marchands de gibier du temple. Miracle de la
jeunesse pâle et furieuse, croyaient-ils.

Il sentit sa main aux mains chargées de bagues et
à la bouche d'un officier; l'officier était à genoux dans
la poudre: et sa tête était assez plaisante, quoique à
demi chaude.

Les voitures filaient dans les étroites rues de la ville;
un mouvement, assez fort pour ce bourg; tout sem-
blait devoir être trop content ce soir-là.

Jésus retira sa main: il eut un mouvement d'orgueil
enfantin et féminin. "Vous autres, si vous ne voyez
pas des miracles, vous ne croyez point."

Jésus n'avait point encore fait de miracles. Il avait,
dans une noce, dans une salle à manger verte et rose,
parlé un peu hautement à la Sainte Vierge. Et per-
sonne n'avait parlé du vin de Cana à Capharnaum,
ni sur le marché, ni sur les quais. Les bourgeois peut-
être.

Jésus dit: "Allez, votre fils se porte bien." L'officier
s'en alla, comme on porte quelque pharmacie légère,

IN GALILEE

Light and charming air of Galilee: the inhabitants received him with curious delight: they had seen him, shaken by holy wrath, driving the money-changers and the merchants of game out of the temple. Miracle of pale and furious youth, they thought.

He felt his hand against the hands, covered with rings, and the mouth of an official; the official was on his knees in the dust: and his looks were pleasing enough, although he was half-bald.

Vehicles were dashing through the narrow streets, rather more activity than usual for this town; everything that evening seemed too satisfied.

Jesus withdrew his hand: it was a movement of childish and feminine pride. "Unless you people see miracles, you don't believe."

Jesus had not yet performed any miracles. He had, at a wedding in a pink and green dining room, spoken rather sharply to the Holy Virgin. And no one, either at the market or on the quays, had mentioned the wine of Cana at Capernaum. Possibly some of the bourgeoisie.

Jesus said: "Go, your son is in good health." The official departed as one who takes with him a light

et Jésus continua par les rues moins fréquentées. Des liserons oranges, des bourraches montraient leur lueur magique entre les pavés. Enfin il vit au loin la prairie poussiéreuse, et les boutons d'or et les marguerites demandant grâce au jour.

A LA PISCINE DE BETH-SAÏDA

Beth-Saïda, la piscine des cinq galeries, était un point d'ennui. Il semblait que ce fût un sinistre lavoir, toujours accablé de la pluie et noir; et les mendiants s'agitant sur les marches intérieures,—blêmies par ces lueurs d'orages précurseurs des éclairs d'enfer, en plaisantant sur leurs yeux bleus aveugles, sur les linges blancs ou bleus dont s'entouraient leurs moignons. O buanderie militaire, ô bain populaire. L'eau était toujours noire, et nul infirme n'y tombait même en songe.

C'est là que Jésus fit la première action grave, avec les infâmes infirmes. Il y avait un jour, de février, mars ou avril, où le soleil de deux heures après-midi laissait s'étaler une grande faux de lumière sur l'eau ensevelie; et comme, là-bas, loin derrière les infirmes, j'aurais pu voir tout ce que ce rayon seul éveillait de bourgeons et de cristaux et de vers, dans ce reflet, pareil à un ange blanc couché sur le côté, tous les reflets infiniment pâles remuaient.

166

stock of drugs, and Jesus went on through the less frequented streets. Between the stones orange bindweed and borage showed their magic light. Finally in the distance he saw the dusty meadow and the buttercups and the daisies begging the day for mercy.

THE POOL OF BETH-SAÏDA

Beth-Saïda, the pool of the five galleries, was a troubled spot. It seemed a sinister washhouse, forever overwhelmed with rain and black: and the beggars, bustling on the inner steps, blanched by the storm glare, harbinger of the lightnings of hell, joking about their blue-blind eyes and the rags of blue and white that bound their stumps. O military laundry! O popular baths! The water was always black and into it no cripple ever fell even in a dream.

It was there that Jesus performed his first serious act, with the crapulous cripples. There was a day in February, March or April, when the sun of two o'clock in the afternoon spread a great sickle of light over the buried waters; and as, back there, far behind the cripples, I might have seen all that this single ray awakened of crystals, buds, and worms, in this beam, like an angel lying on its side, all the infinitely pale reflections stirred.

Tous les péchés, fils légers et tenaces du démon, qui, pour les cœurs un peu sensibles, rendaient ces hommes plus effrayants que les monstres, voulaient se jeter à cette eau. Les infirmes descendirent, ne raillant plus, mais avec envie.

Les premiers entrés sortaient guéris, disait-on. Non. Les péchés les rejetaient sur les marches, et les forçaient de chercher d'autres postes: car leur Démon ne peut rester qu'aux lieux où l'aumône est sûre.

Jésus entra aussitôt après l'heure de midi. Personne ne lavait ni ne descendait de bêtes. La lumière dans la piscine était jaune comme les dernières feuilles des vignes. Le divin maître se tenait contre une colonne: il regardait les fils du Péché; le démon tirait sa langue en leur langue, et riait au monde.

Le Paralytique se leva, qui était resté couché sur le flanc, et ce fut d'un pas singulièrement assuré qu'ils le virent franchir la galerie et disparaître dans la ville, les Damnés.

All the sins, light and obstinate sons of the demon who, for somewhat impressionable hearts, made these men more horrible than monsters, wanted to throw themselves into this water. The cripples descended, no longer jeering, but with envy.

The first to enter would come out cured, they said. No. The sins threw them back upon the steps, and forced them to look for other places: for their demon can only stay where charity is sure.

Jesus entered just after the hour of noon. No one was washing or watering beasts. The light of the pool was yellow like the last leaves of the vine. The divine master leaned against a column: he looked at the sons of Sin: the demon stuck out his tongue in their tongue, and laughed at the world.

The paralytic, who was lying on his side, rose. And they, the Damned, saw that it was with a singularly firm step that he crossed the gallery and disappeared into the city.

NOTES ON SOME CORRECTIONS
AND REVISIONS

Page 21. *Side Show: On les envoie prendre du dos en ville.* . . .
Prendre du dos is defined in Emile Chautard's *La Vie Étrange de
l'Argot* (1931) as "active pederasty." Rimbaud's sentence might be
translated: "They are sent buggering in town." But, since I found
that not all literate Frenchmen are familiar with this slang expres-
sion—and perhaps in Rimbaud's day it was understood only by
voyous like himself—I hardly think so exact and familiar a word
in English would be an equivalent. "To snare," also a slang ex-
pression, which may or may not be understood, is defined as "to
secure a catamite."

Page 25. *Antique:* See note on *H.*

Page 29. *Lives:* . . . *la main de la campagne sur mon épaule,* etc.
The previous edition read *la compagne* (companion, feminine,
which I formerly translated "girl"). There is no doubt about the
word in the manuscript: it is *campagne.* But someone, not Rim-
baud, probably the first editor, Fénéon, penciled an "o" over the
"a." With the exception of Bouillane de Lacoste, all editors since
have accepted this correction, the editors of La Pléiade finding it
"obvious." De Lacoste alone does not agree that the "a" was a slip
of the pen. He feels that the phrase is a characteristic Rimbaud
personification, and cites several examples, among others from
*Aube: je l'ai entourée avec ses voiles amassés, et j'ai senti un peu
son immense corps.* I am still a little dubious, not because of the

"hand of the country on my shoulder," which is charming, but the rest of the image, "standing etc.," strikes me as rather labored for Rimbaud. I hesitated. Then I thought of the peculiar intimacy between Rimbaud and the country, expressed over and over again ever since he was a schoolboy and wrote in one of his Latin poems: ... *pectusque calentis insinuabat amor ruris* (... and into my breast crept the love of the warm country). Just another dilemma for the obsessed translator of Rimbaud.

Page 55. *The Bridges:* The title, which was inadvertently omitted in the first edition and by subsequent editors, is here restored.

Page 68. *Cities:* ... *plus fiers que des***.* In the manuscript a word is crossed out and another written over it. De Lacoste, after first thinking the inserted word might be *Bravi,* now concludes that both words are indecipherable and uses asterisks. Berrichon gave *Brennus;* La Pléiade reads *brahmans.* Such divergent guessing makes me prefer asterisks.

Page 75. *Vigils:* In the manuscript, *Veillées* has only three parts. Berrichon added a fourth, taking it from the end of *Jeunesse.* It will here be found in its proper place.

Page 90. *Marine:* Although written on the same page as *Fête D'Hiver,* it was formerly classified as one of the late verse poems.

Page 93. *Winter Fête:* Not only was the title omitted in early editions, but, in some of them, the poem was printed as part of *Marine.* Berrichon, in his 1912 edition, separated it from *Marine* only to tack it on to *Phrases.* It is here given its original status as a separate poem.

Page 123. *H.* Formerly this poem was incorrectly entitled "Antique II." De Lacoste offers the following explanation of how the title "H" disappeared: After several printings the letter "H" became so worn that it lost its crossbar and became the Roman numeral II. Someone then decided that it must be the sequel to the preceding poem which, in Berrichon's order, was *Antique,* hence "Antique II."

Page 125. *Devotions:* ... *du temps des Amies* (the Friends, feminine). This, I now believe, is a reference to the little book of erotic sonnets by Verlaine, *Les Amies,* written under the pseudonym Pablo Maria Herlagnez, and published in Brussels in 1867, by the publisher of Baudelaire's *Les Fleurs du Mal,* Poulet-Mallasis, who

NOTES ON CORRECTIONS AND REVISIONS

specialized in erotic, not to say pornographic, literature. It cannot be translated into the neutral English, "The Friends," without losing the obvious though veiled implication of the paragraph.

...*son cœur ambre et spunk.* The first edition read "spunck"; Berrichon later changed it to "spunsk"; La Pléiade has "skunk," and de Lacoste, "spunk." In a letter to Berrichon, Fénéon wrote: "Neither 'spunck' nor 'spunsk' exists in English, but 'spunk' does, meaning flint and, figuratively, in colloquial speech, courage, heart, fire, mettle." Berrichon evidently did not adopt this suggestion. De Lacoste did, and so do I. Rimbaud perhaps thought of the meaning flint, but with all the overtones of spunk. There may have been a "c" in the manuscript—Rimbaud's misspelling, or the printer's, of an English word. Since this manuscript is missing, one is forced to guess.

Page 133. *War:* This poem appeared in the former New Directions edition as Part IV of *Youth,* a mistake which occurred in several Berrichon editions. It is written on a separate sheet of the manuscript.

Page 163. *Gospel Moralities:* The first two poems are taken from the fourth chapter of the Gospel of St. John, with reference to incidents in Chapter 2; and *Beth-Saïda,* from Chapter 5. There is a slight discrepancy between de Lacoste's reading of the first poem and that of Jacques Gengoux in his *Pensée Poétique de Rimbaud.* I have followed Gengoux since he has deciphered several words de Lacoste found illegible. Both print in brackets words that are crossed out in the manuscript: *Samarie [s'enorgueillsait], la parvenue [la perfide]* ... (Samaria [was puffed up with pride] the upstart [the perfidious] ...). The manuscripts of these three poems are obviously rough drafts, though by no means so disorderly and confused as the first drafts of *Une Saison en Enfer.* I feel certain that had Rimbaud made a final copy, even without changing the text, he would have corrected two manifest slips of the pen. The first is in the poem *In Samaria:* Rimbaud wrote, *"vous êtes prophètes"* instead of, as in the gospel story, *"vous êtes un prophète."* Considering how faithfully Rimbaud, for all his impious juggleries and delicious descriptive additions, followed the Bible stories in these poems, I feel justified in dropping the plural. Perhaps it is this apparent orthodoxy of Rimbaud's that accounts

172

for the cecity of his evangelic exegetes (none so blind ... as the saying goes) which has led them in their interpretations of *Beth-Saïda* to ignore Rimbaud's irreverence. Only Etiemble and Yasu Gauclerc have shown the full blasphemous significance of this bitter poem. The other slip is in the second poem: *"demi chaude"* (half-hot, which is nonsense) instead of *"demi-chauve"* (half-bald). I have taken the liberty of making these two corrections.

A RIMBAUD CHRONOLOGY

The following is based on the chronology compiled by Wallace Fowlie for his Rimbaud: The Myth of Childhood *(New York: New Directions, 1946), with additional data taken from Dr. Enid Starkie's* Arthur Rimbaud *(New York: W. W. Norton & Co., 1947) and her Zaharoff lecture,* Arthur Rimbaud, 1854–1954 *(Oxford: Clarendon Press, 1954).*

1854
Jean-Nicolas-Arthur Rimbaud is born on October 20 at Charleville (Ardennes).

1860
His parents separate, the children remaining in the mother's charge.

1862
He enters school.

1865

Enters *7ième* class, Collège de Charleville, where he shows virtuosity in Latin verse.

1869

In October he is writing poetry in French.

1870

Publishes his first poem in *Revue pour Tous* in January; on May 24 he writes to Théodore de Banville and sends him several poems; in July the Franco-Prussian War breaks out. Rimbaud graduates from the Collège on August 6, and on the 28th runs off to Paris by train. He is arrested for having no ticket or money. His former teacher, Georges Izambard, helps secure his release; Rimbaud visits Izambard at Douai and trains with Garde Nationale for three weeks; he returns to Charleville on September 27; and on October 7 runs off to Belgium (Charleroi, Brussels); he returns to Izambard at Douai; on October 29 is back in Charleville. Mézières is bombarded on December 20, and it and neighboring Charleville are occupied by the Prussians.

1871

On February 25 he makes third flight, to Paris, where he hopes to join Garde Nationale; he stays

with André Gill; on March 10 returns to Charleville. The Commune is established on the 28th; he may have been in Paris April 17. During this period Collège de Charleville is closed because of the war; Rimbaud and school friend Ernest Delahaye take long walks on which Rimbaud reads his poems, including *Les Déserts de l'Amour*. From Charleville he writes first *"Lettre du Voyant"* to Izambard on May 13, and the second, to Paul Demeny, on May 15; in these letters Rimbaud expounds his theory of poetry and how to become a poet or "voyant," through the disordering of all the senses. Comes under influence of Charles Bretagne, customs official, amateur musician and occultist who is friend of Verlaine. At his suggestion, in August Rimbaud writes Verlaine, enclosing some of his poems; Verlaine summons him to Paris, which he reaches in late September. After staying with Verlaine two weeks, and other friends for a time, he takes a room, paid for by Verlaine, on rue Campagne-Première.

1872

Rimbaud sets out to shock the writers and artists in Verlaine's circle; the relations of Verlaine and Rimbaud become the subject of gossip, and Verlaine persuades Rimbaud to return to Charleville to quiet his wife's suspicions. In May Verlaine sends Rim-

baud money and he goes back to Paris. On July 7 he leaves with Verlaine for Brussels; they depart for England on September 8, reaching London on the 10th. Mme. Verlaine prepares suit for separation and Mme. Rimbaud attempts to intervene. In late December Rimbaud is back in Charleville.

1873

Verlaine, ill in London, calls back Rimbaud, who reaches London in January; on April 4 they go to Brussels, and on the 11th Rimbaud returns to mother's farm at Roche (near Charleville) where he begins *Une Saison en Enfer*. On May 27 Verlaine and Rimbaud return to England; in late June, after quarrels, Verlaine leaves for Belgium. He sends Rimbaud money to come to him and Rimbaud reaches Brussels on July 8. On July 10 Rimbaud tells Verlaine he is leaving for Paris; Verlaine fires revolver at him and hits him in wrist; when Verlaine again threatens him, Rimbaud goes to the police for protection and Verlaine is arrested. On July 17 the bullet is extracted, and on the 19th Rimbaud attempts to withdraw charges, without success. He returns to Roche on the 20th; Verlaine is sentenced to two years in prison on August 8. This month Rimbaud finishes *Une Saison en Enfer,* and has it printed.

1874

Rimbaud meets Germain Nouveau in Paris in February. In March they are in London together. The existing manuscript of *Illuminations,* evidently a copy, dates from this period (see Introduction). His mother and sister visit him there; on July 31 Rimbaud goes to Reading to teach; in late December he returns to Charleville.

1875

Rimbaud goes to Stuttgart to learn German. Verlaine is released from prison in January; he and Rimbaud meet in Stuttgart in February; Rimbaud crosses Alps on foot, visits Milan, sails to Paris, returns to Marseille; in August he returns to Paris, then to Charleville, where he studies languages. He takes up the piano and becomes interested in science. In December his sister Vitalie dies.

1876

After quarrels with his mother and brother he goes to Vienna, then to Holland where he joins the Dutch army and sails for Dutch East Indies in June; he deserts in Java in August, and is back in Charleville by December 31.

1877

In the spring he goes to Hamburg, then takes ship for Alexandria, but is landed in Italy because of illness. He returns to Charleville.

1878

In October he goes to Hamburg, then to Genoa where he takes ship for Alexandria; then goes to Cyprus as foreman over work gang in quarry.

1879

After typhoid fever, he returns to Roche in June.

1880

Returns to Cyprus; quarrels with his employers; travels down Red Sea in June; in August is in Aden working in coffee exporter's store. In December he reaches Harar where he sets up branch trading post.

1881

Returns to Aden in December.

1883

Returns to Harar, and makes a journey of exploration into a part of Ogaden where no European had penetrated previously. Verlaine publishes some of

Rimbaud's poems in an article on him in *Lutece* (October, November; republished in 1884 in his *Les Poètes maudits*).

1884

Société de Géographie publishes Rimbaud's report on the province of Ogaden, in February. In September Egypt evacuates Harar; and Rimbaud returns to Aden with, it is said, an Harari girl whom he sends back to Abyssinia in October, 1885.

1886

In October Rimbaud goes to Tajoura to engage in arms trade. *Illuminations* published in *La Vogue,* and in book form, as by "the late Arthur Rimbaud," with an introduction by Verlaine.

1887

Rimbaud's caravan reaches Entoto in February; he sells his cargo of arms to King Menelek of Shoa in May, is bested in the bargain; returns to Aden, goes to Cairo for the summer, and returns to Aden in the autumn.

1888

In May he goes to Harar to direct a trading station.

writes his mother for scientific books. Verlaine pub-
lishes second article on Rimbaud in *Les Hommes
d'aujourd'hui*.

1891
Suffering from growth on his knee and fever, Rim-
baud is carried by litter to Zeyla and takes boat to
Aden in April; on May 2 he reaches Marseille; his
mother visits him in hospital; his leg is amputated.
The disease is diagnosed as carcinoma. In July he
goes to Roche, and in August returns to hospital in
Marseille, accompanied by his sister, Isabelle. He
dies on November 10 and his body is returned to
Charleville for burial. Before dying, he asked to
have 3,000 francs sent to Djami, the Harari boy
who had been his body servant and constant com-
panion for eight years. In this month Rodolphe
Darzens publishes the first important collection of
Rimbaud's poems.

New Directions Paperbooks—A Partial Listing

Walter Abish, *How German Is It.* NDP508.
John Allman, *Scenarios for a Mixed Landscape.* NDP619.
Sherwood Anderson, *Poor White.* NDP763.
Wayne Andrews, *The Surrealist Parade.* NDP689.
David Antin, *Tuning.* NDP570.
G. Apollinaire, *Selected Writings.*† NDP310.
Jimmy S. Baca, *Martín & Meditations.* NDP648.
Black Mesa Poems. NDP676.
Djuna Barnes, *Nightwood.* NDP98.
J. Barzun, *An Essay on French Verse.* NDP708.
H.E. Bates, *Elephant's Nest in a Rhubarb Tree.* NDP669.
A Party for the Girls, NDP653.
Charles Baudelaire, *Flowers of Evil.*† NDP684.
Paris Spleen. NDP294.
Bei Dao, *Old Snow.* NDP727.
Waves. NDP693.
Gottfried Benn, *Primal Vision.* NDP322.
Adolfo Bioy Casares, *A Russian Doll.* NDP745.
Carmel Bird, *The Bluebird Café.* NDP707.
R. P. Blackmur, *Studies in Henry James,* NDP552.
Wolfgang Borchert, *The Man Outside.* NDP319.
Jorge Luis Borges, *Labyrinths.* NDP186.
Seven Nights. NDP576.
Kay Boyle, *Life Being the Best.* NDP654.
Fifty Stories. NDP741.
M. Bulgakov, *Flight & Bliss.* NDP593.
The Life of M. de Moliere. NDP601.
Frederick Busch, *Absent Friends.* NDP721.
Veza Canetti, *Yellow Street.* NDP709.
Ernesto Cardenal, *Zero Hour.* NDP502.
Joyce Cary, *A House of Children.* NDP631.
Mister Johnson. NDP631.
Hayden Carruth, *Tell Me Again. . . .* NDP677.
Louis-Ferdinand Céline,
Death on the Installment Plan. NDP330.
Journey to the End of the Night. NDP542.
René Char. *Selected Poems.*† NDP734.
Jean Cocteau, *The Holy Terrors.* NDP212.
M. Collis, *She Was a Queen.* NDP716.
Cid Corman, *Sun Rock Man.* NDP318.
Gregory Corso, *Long Live Man.* NDP127.
Herald of the Autochthonic Spirit. NDP522.
Robert Creeley, *Memory Gardens.* NDP613.
Windows. NDP687.
Edward Dahlberg, *Because I Was Flesh.* NDP227.
Alain Daniélou, *The Way to the Labyrinth.* NDP634.
Osamu Dazai, *The Setting Sun.* NDP258.
No Longer Human. NDP357.
Mme. de Lafayette, *The Princess of Cleves.* NDP660.
E. Dujardin, *We'll to the Woods No More.* NDP682.
Robert Duncan, *Selected Poems.* NDP754.
Richard Eberhart, *The Long Reach.* NDP565.
Wm. Empson, *7 Types of Ambiguity.* NDP204.
Some Versions of Pastoral. NDP92.
S. Endo, *The Sea and the Poison.* NDP737.
Wm. Everson, *The Residual Years.* NDP263.
Gavin Ewart, *Selected Poems.* NDP655.
Lawrence Ferlinghetti, *A Coney Island of the Mind.* NDP74.
Starting from San Francisco. NDP220.
Wild Dreams of a New Beginning. NDP663.
Ronald Firbank, *Five Novels.* NDP581.
Three More Novels. NDP614.
F. Scott Fitzgerald, *The Crack-up.* NDP54.
Gustave Flaubert, *Dictionary.* NDP230.
J. Gahagan, *Did Gustav Mahler Ski?* NDP711.
Gandhi, *Gandhi on Non-Violence.* NDP197.
Gary, Romain, *Promise at Dawn.* NDP635.
The Life Before Us ("Madame Rosa"). NDP604.
W. Gerhardie, *Futility.* NDP722.
Goethe, *Faust,* Part I. NDP70.
Allen Grossman, *The Ether Dome.* NDP723.
Martin Grzimek, *Shadowlife.* NDP705.
Guigonnat, Henri, *Daemon in Lithuania.* NDP592.
Lars Gustafsson, *The Death of a Beekeeper.* NDP523.
A Tiler's Afternoon. NDP761.

John Hawkes, *The Beetle Leg.* NDP239.
. Humors of Blood & Skin. NDP577.
Second Skin. NDP146.
Samuel Hazo, *To Paris.* NDP512.
H. D. *Collected Poems.* NDP611.
Helen in Egypt. NDP380.
HERmione. NDP526.
Selected Poems. NDP658.
Tribute to Freud. NDP572.
Robert E. Helbling, *Heinrich von Kleist.* NDP390.
William Herrick, *Bradovich.* NDP762.
Herman Hesse, *Siddhartha.* NDP65.
Paul Hoover, *The Novel.* NDP706.
Susan Howe, *The Nonconformist's Memorial.* NDP755.
Vicente Huidobro, *Selected Poetry.* NDP520.
C. Isherwood, *All the Conspirators.* NDP480.
The Berlin Stories. NDP134.
Ledo Ivo, *Snake's Nest.* NDP521.
Fleur Jaeggy, *Sweet Days of Discipline.* NDP758.
Gustav Janouch, *Conversations with Kafka.* NDP313.
Alfred Jarry, *Ubu Roi.* NDP105.
Robinson Jeffers, *Cawdor and Medea.* NDP293.
B.S. Johnson, *Christie Malry's. . . .* NDP600.
Albert Angelo. NDP628.
James Joyce, *Stephen Hero.* NDP133.
Franz Kafka, *Amerika.* NDP117.
Mary Karr, *The Devil's Tour.* NDP768.
Bob Kaufman, *The Ancient Rain.* NDP514.
H. von Kleist, *Prince Friedrich.* NDP462.
Rüdiger Kremer, *The Color of Snow.* NDP743.
Jules Laforgue, *Moral Tales.* NDP594.
P. Lal, *Great Sanskrit Plays.* NDP142.
Tommaso Landolfi, *Gogol's Wife.* NDP155.
"Language" Poetries: An Anthology. NDP630.
D. Larsen, *Stitching Porcelain.* NDP710.
James Laughlin, *The Man in the Wall.* NDP759.
Lautréamont, *Maldoror.* NDP207.
H. Leibowitz, *Fabricating Lives.* NDP715.
Siegfried Lenz, *The German Lesson.* NDP618.
Denise Levertov, *Breathing the Water.* NDP640.
A Door in the Hive. NDP685.
Evening Train. NDP750.
New & Selected Essays. NDP749.
Poems 1960-1967. NDP549.
Poems 1968-1972. NDP629.
Oblique Prayers. NDP578.
Harry Levin, *James Joyce.* NDP87.
Li Ch'ing-chao, *Complete Poems.* NDP492.
Enrique Lihn, *The Dark Room.*† NDP542.
C. Lispector, *Soulstorm.* NDP671.
The Hour of the Star. NDP733.
Garciá Lorca, *Five Plays.* NDP232.
The Public & Play Without a Title. NDP561.
Selected Poems.† NDP114.
Three Tragedies. NDP52.
Francisco G. Lorca, *In The Green Morning.* NDP610.
Michael McClure, *Rebel Lions.* NDP712.
Selected Poems. NDP599.
Carson McCullers, *The Member of the Wedding.* (Playscript) NDP153.
Stéphane Mallarme,† *Selected Poetry and Prose.* NDP529.
Bernadette Mayer, *A Bernadette Mayer Reader.* NDP739.
Thomas Merton, *Asian Journal.* NDP394.
New Seeds of Contemplation. ND337.
Selected Poems. NDP85.
Thomas Merton in Alaska. NDP652.
The Way of Chuang Tzu. NDP276.
Zen and the Birds of Appetite. NDP261.
Henri Michaux, *A Barbarian in Asia.* NDP622.
Selected Writings. NDP264.
Henry Miller, *The Air-Conditioned Nightmare.* NDP302.
Aller Retour New York. NDP753.
Big Sur & The Oranges. NDP161.
The Colossus of Maroussi. NDP75.
A Devil in Paradise. NDP765.
Into the Heart of Life. NDP728.
The Smile at the Foot of the Ladder. NDP386.

For complete listing request free catalog from
New Directions, 80 Eighth Avenue, New York 10011

†Bilingual

Y. Mishima, *Confessions of a Mask*. NDP253.
 Death in Midsummer. NDP215.
Frédéric Mistral, *The Memoirs*. NDP632.
Eugenio Montale, *It Depends.*† NDP507.
 Selected Poems.† NDP193.
Paul Morand, *Fancy Goods / Open All Night.*
 NDP567.
Vladimir Nabokov, *Nikolai Gogol*. NDP78.
 Laughter in the Dark. NDP729.
 The Real Life of Sebastian Knight. NDP432.
P. Neruda, *The Captain's Verses.*† NDP345.
 Residence on Earth.† NDP340.
New Directions in Prose & Poetry (Anthology).
 Available from #17 forward to #55.
Robert Nichols, *Arrival*. NDP437.
 Exile. NDP485.
J. F. Nims, *The Six-Cornered Snowflake*. NDP700.
Charles Olson, *Selected Writings*. NDP231.
Toby Olson, *The Life of Jesus*. NDP417.
 Seaview. NDP532.
George Oppen, *Collected Poems*. NDP418.
István Örkeny, *The Flower Show /*
 The Toth Family. NDP536.
Wilfred Owen, *Collected Poems*. NDP210.
José Emilio Pacheco, *Battles in the Desert*. NDP637.
 Selected Poems.† NDP638.
Nicanor Parra, *Antipoems: New & Selected*. NDP603.
Boris Pasternak, *Safe Conduct*. NDP77.
Kenneth Patchen, *Because It Is*. NDP83.
 Collected Poems. NDP284.
 Selected Poems. NDP160.
 Wonderings. NDP320.
Ota Pavel, *How I Came to Know Fish*. NDP713.
Octavio Paz, *Collected Poems*. NDP719.
 Configurations.† NDP303.
 A Draft of Shadows.† NDP489.
 Selected Poems. NDP574.
 Sunstone.† NDP735.
 A Tree Within.† NDP661.
St. John Perse, *Selected Poems.*† NDP545.
J. A. Porter, *Eelgrass*. NDP438.
Ezra Pound, *ABC of Reading*. NDP89.
 Confucius. NDP285.
 Confucius to Cummings. (Anth.) NDP126.
 A Draft of XXX Cantos. NDP690.
 Elektra. NDP683.
 Guide to Kulchur. NDP257.
 Literary Essays. NDP250.
 Personae. NDP697.
 Selected Cantos. NDP304.
 Selected Poems. NDP66.
 The Spirit of Romance. NDP266.
Raymond Queneau, *The Blue Flowers*. NDP595.
 Exercises in Style. NDP513.
Mary de Rachewiltz, *Ezra Pound*. NDP405.
Raja Rao, *Kanthapura*. NDP224.
Herbert Read, *The Green Child*. NDP208.
P. Reverdy, *Selected Poems.*† NDP346.
Kenneth Rexroth, *An Autobiographical Novel*. NDP725.
 Classics Revisited. NDP621.
 More Classics Revisited. NDP668.
 Flower Wreath Hill. NDP724.
 100 Poems from the Chinese. NDP192.
 100 Poems from the Japanese.† NDP147.
 Selected Poems. NDP581.
 Women Poets of China. NDP528.
 Women Poets of Japan. NDP527.
Rainer Maria Rilke, *Poems from*
 The Book of Hours. NDP408.
 Possibility of Being. (Poems). NDP436.
 Where Silence Reigns. (Prose). NDP464.
Arthur Rimbaud, *Illuminations.*† NDP56.
 Season in Hell & Drunken Boat.† NDP97.
Edouard Roditi, *Delights of Turkey*. NDP445.
Jerome Rothenberg, *Khurbn*. NDP679.
 New Selected Poems. NDP625.
Nayantara Sahgal, *Rich Like Us*. NDP665.

Ihara Saikaku, *The Life of an Amorous*
 Woman. NDP270.
St. John of the Cross, *Poems.*† NDP341.
W. Saroyan, *Man With the Heart in the Highlands.*
 NDP740.
Jean-Paul Sartre, *Nausea*. NDP82.
 The Wall (Intimacy). NDP272.
P. D. Scott, *Coming to Jakarta*. NDP672.
 Listening to the Candle. NDP747.
Delmore Schwartz, *Selected Poems*. NDP241.
 In Dreams Begin Responsibilities. NDP454.
Shattan, *Manimekhalaï*. NDP674.
K. Shiraishi. *Seasons of Sacred Lust*. NDP453.
Stevie Smith, *Collected Poems*. NDP562.
 New Selected Poems. NDP659.
Gary Snyder, *The Back Country*. NDP249.
 The Real Work. NDP499.
 Regarding Wave. NDP306.
 Turtle Island. NDP381.
Muriel Spark, *The Public Image*. NDP767.
Enid Starkie, *Rimbaud*. NDP254.
Stendhal. *Three Italian Chronicles*. NDP704.
Antonio Tabucchi, *Indian Nocturne*. NDP666.
Nathaniel Tarn, *Lyrics . . . Bride of God*. NDP391.
Dylan Thomas, *Adventures in the Skin Trade.*
 NDP183.
 A Child's Christmas in Wales. NDP181.
 Collected Poems 1934-1952. NDP316.
 Collected Stories. NDP626.
 Portrait of the Artist as a Young Dog. NDP51.
 Quite Early One Morning. NDP90.
 Under Milk Wood. NDP73.
Tian Wen: *A Chinese Book of Origins*. NDP624.
Uwe Timm, *The Snake Tree*. NDP686.
Lionel Trilling, *E. M. Forster*. NDP189.
Tu Fu, *Selected Poems*. NDP675.
N. Tucci, *The Rain Came Last*. NDP688.
Paul Valéry, *Selected Writings.*† NDP184.
Elio Vittorini, *A Vittorini Omnibus*. NDP366.
Rosmarie Waldrop, *The Reproduction of Profiles.*
 NDP649.
Robert Penn Warren, *At Heaven's Gate*. NDP588.
Vernon Watkins, *Selected Poems*. NDP221.
Eliot Weinberger, *Outside Stories*. NDP /51.
Nathanael West, *Miss Lonelyhearts &*
 Day of the Locust. NDP125.
J. Wheelwright, *Collected Poems*. NDP544.
Tennessee Williams, *Baby Doll*. NDP714.
 Camino Real. NDP301.
 Cat on a Hot Tin Roof. NDP398.
 Clothes for a Summer Hotel. NDP556.
 The Glass Menagerie. NDP218.
 Hard Candy. NDP225.
 A Lovely Sunday for Creve Coeur. NDP497.
 One Arm & Other Stories. NDP237.
 Red Devil Battery Sign. NDP650.
 A Streetcar Named Desire. NDP501.
 Sweet Bird of Youth. NDP409.
 Twenty-Seven Wagons Full of Cotton. NDP217.
 Vieux Carre. NDP482.
William Carlos Williams,
 The Autobiography. NDP223.
 The Buildup. NDP259.
 Collected Poems: Vol. I. NDP730
 Collected Poems: Vol. II. NDP731
 The Doctor Stories. NDP585.
 Imaginations. NDP329.
 In the American Grain. NDP53.
 In the Money. NDP240.
 Paterson. Complete. NDP152.
 Pictures from Brueghel. NDP118.
 Selected Poems (new ed.). NDP602.
 White Mule. NDP226.
Wisdom Books: *Spanish Mystics*. NDP442;
 St. Francis. NDP477; *Taoists*. NDP509;
 Wisdom of the Desert. NDP295;
 Zen Masters. NDP415.

For complete listing request free catalog from
New Directions, 80 Eighth Avenue, New York 10011

†Bilingual